IDIOTS IN PARIS

DIARIES OF J.G. BENNETT
AND ELIZABETH BENNETT
1949

IDIOTS IN PARIS: The Diaries of J.G. Bennett and Elizabeth Bennett

Originally published Coombe Springs Press 1980
This edition published by the J.G. Bennett Foundation

© The Estate of J.G. Bennett and Elizabeth Bennett 2016
All rights reserved

ISBN-13: 978-1541113923

ISBN-10: 1541113926

Foreword

THE PUBLICATION of a personal diary is a hazardous business, whether or not the writer is still living. Equally, such a diary written with an eye on possible future readers is an absurdity. These two interlocking diaries were written for the writers alone - to clarify thoughts, and to record details that we might refer to in the future and which we could otherwise have forgotten. One cannot edit such diaries by incorporating explanations in the text and so on, without making them artificial and leaving the reader uncertain of the writer's credibility. Moreover, I personally dislike footnotes and have therefore made a minimal use of them. I am left with only one practical resource - this rather long explanatory preface. It is designed to help those readers who are not familiar with the activities and environment of Gurdjieff and his followers, giving them some picture not only of the stage on which his last days were played, but also of the background of the writers of the diaries.

So then.

The philosopher George Ivanovitch Gurdjieff left Russia with some of his followers during the Revolution and after long and difficult wanderings settled in France, at the Château du Prieuré at Avon, outside Fontainebleau. He lived here, with pupils from many parts of the world, for some years, until his career there was brought to an end by a motor accident, which almost cost him his life. He then turned his attention to writing, and produced his inspired masterpiece, 'All and Everything'. This work has a subtitle, 'Beelzebub's Tales to his Grandson' and throughout the diaries, the book, which was then in manuscript form, is referred to as Beelzebub or sometimes, if Gurdjieff is the speaker, as "first série my writing." There are two other books, since published, referred to simply as 'second' and 'third series'.

Gurdjieff settled finally in Paris. With the outbreak of the War in 1939, he lost touch with those of his followers who were centreed around J.G. Bennett, who did not even know if he was alive, though some other groups of his students managed to maintain some kind of contact with him.

J.G. Bennett, who, during the war was engaged in industrial research, had met Gurdjieff in Constantinople and at the Prieuré, and regarded him as his teacher. When the War ended he set up a centre at Kingston-upon-Thames for the study of man as a psychokinetic being, the studies being based on the psychological system taught by Gurdjieff. This centre was established at Coombe Springs, an Edwardian villa with seven acres of land. There were about twenty residents and many short-term visitors. I went to live there at the end of my war-time service, and was able to study Gurdjieff's psychological and cosmological ideas and also to begin work on the "Movements." These Movements were a system of dances or sacred gymnastics on which Gurdjieff placed much emphasis and which, among other things, enabled the pupil to observe himself as a three-natured being and as a whole. Of course I was not married to J.G. Bennett at that time. The Mrs. B who appears in the text is his second wife, Winifred Alice Bennett, known affectionately as Polly.

While I was living at Coombe Springs, in 1948, J.G. Bennett, with the help of Madame Ouspensky, renewed his contact with Gurdjieff. She was the widow of P. D. Ouspensky, author of 'Tertium Organum', 'A New Model of the Universe', and 'In Search of the Miraculous'. I was in Paris in August of that year and so met Gurdjieff for the first time. In January 1949, I had a mild nervous breakdown as a result of seeing too much too soon, and Mr. Bennett, unable to help me himself, sent me to Paris to be near Gurdjieff. So it happened that I was launched into this strange, satisfying environment, at once ritually stylized and perpetually fluid, where Gurdjieff gave me permission to live and where I quickly recovered my emotional and physical stability. I kept a somewhat haphazard diary of my arrival and first few months in Paris, but this volume was accidentally destroyed. The second volume, published here, plunges without ceremony into the life which then revolved

FOREWORD

around Gurdjieff's flat in the Rue des Colonels Renard.

It is necessary to give some explanation here of the daily routine and the terms in general use, as there is no explanation in the text. I am concerned only with Gurdjieff's day-to-day life in his flat, not with his work in Paris as a whole, of which I knew little or nothing. The days at the flat were always the same, unless, of course, Gurdjieff went away for a few days' relaxation in some other part of France, as he is about to do at the start of my own diary. In the summer of 1949, large numbers of people were coming to Paris to visit him, and these people were all invited to the flat for lunch or dinner, or both. There were also many members of his French groups, his household of near people and relations, and finally, one or two long-term visitors like myself. We would go to lunch at midday. There was always a reading aloud of some part of Gurdjieff's own writings, or occasionally from P. D. Ouspensky's 'In Search of the Miraculous', called throughout the diaries 'Fragments', a reference to Ouspensky's original choice of a title. The reading would last for one or two hours and then we would go to the dining room for lunch. As there was very little space, the plates were passed from the Kitchen to the dining room by a *chaine* formed usually by the young people, or *habitués*, while the new guests and older people went straight into the room. The room was small and usually so packed with people that once one had found a place, one would remain wedged until the meal was over, it was not possible to get out again. Once the seats at the table were filled, and those at the little side-table, people would stand behind the chairs or sit on little stools crammed into a corner, in the fireplace and so on, while people ate with their plates on their knees, or on the chimney-piece or the piano or wherever they could.

The arrangement of the table was formal. Gurdjieff sat at the far end and beside him on his left was the Director of the feast. The Director had to see that everything went smoothly, that no one was without food or drink, and so on. He had to look after Mr. Gurdjieff, changing his plates and carrying out his instructions about various details, giving the Toasts in a clear voice when the time came. The ritual of the Toasts was drawn from what Gurdjieff called the "Science of Idiotism." He explained that in a Sufi community, "... a method of teaching had been handed down from antiquity which consisted in tracing the path of man's evolution from a state of nature to the realization of his spiritual potential .... There are twenty-one gradations of reason from that of the ordinary man to that of Our Endlessness, that is, God. No one can reach the Absolute Reason of God, and only the sons of God like Jesus Christ can have the two gradations of reason that are nineteenth and twentieth. Therefore, the aim of every being who aspires to perfection must be to reach the eighteenth gradation .... The word idiot has two meanings: the true meaning that was given to it by the ancient sages was *to be oneself.* A man who is himself looks and behaves like a madman to those who live in the world of illusions, so when they call a man an idiot they mean that he does not share their illusions. Everyone who decides to work on himself is an idiot in both meanings. The wise know that he is seeking for reality. The foolish think he has taken leave of his senses. We here are supposed to be seeking for reality, so we should all be idiots: but no one can make you an idiot. You must choose it for yourself. That is why everyone who visits us here and wishes to remain in contact with us, is allowed to choose his own idiotism. Then all the rest of us will wish from our hearts that he will truly become that idiot. For this alcohol was used by the ancient sages; not to get drunk, but to strengthen the power to wish".[1] He made constant use of the idiots in his teaching.

On the Director's left sat the man responsible for pouring drinks and distributing them to the guests. He was known as the pourer or *Verseur*. He had to remember what each person was drinking, so that each glass could be refilled correctly when the time came. At right-angles to Mr. Gurdjieff, at the narrow end of the table on his right, sat *Monsieur Egout*. "Egout" means a drain or sewer, and this position was usually occupied by what Gurdjieff called an "esteemed person." He was given, in addition to his own plate, various extra foods and

[1] J.G. Bennett, "*Gurdjieff: Making a New World*"

tidbits by Mr. Gurdjieff, and these of course he was bound to eat. If he was given more than he could eat, he was allowed to pass his own plate, or some part of its contents, to *Monsieur Poubelle* (dustbin) on his right. Round the corner of the table, at Poubelle's right and therefore opposite to Mr. Gurdjieff, sat *Bouche d'Egout*, the "mouth of the sewer." He was often offered various *bonne-bouches* by Mr. Gurdjieff across the table. *Egout pour Sweet* had a special function - to eat Mr. Gurdjieff's pudding or dessert if he did not want it himself. He would call for *Egout pour Sweet* if he needed her, and from whatever place she was occupying she would reply, "*présente, Monsieur,*" and come forward for her treat. This rôle was usually played by a young woman.

The ritual was repeated exactly in the evening. Twice every day we participated in the reading, the *chaine*, the meal, the Toasts, the music. The flat looked exactly the same at all times; by day and by night the shutters were closed and the electric lights burning. After a time one ceased to know whether it was night or day. More than once after a meal I have emerged blinking into the hot summer sunshine in the street, when I had expected lamp-lit darkness, or been surprised by darkness when I had expected daylight. The exact repetition of the external framework left one free to attend to the shifting possibilities of the inner world. Every moment in Gurdjieff's presence was a chance to learn, if one was sufficiently awake to take the chance.

There were several young American women there, who had come to Paris to study the Movements, with the intention that they should return to teach them in America. Among them were Tanya Savitsky, Madame Ouspensky's grand-daughter, and Iovanna Lloyd Wright, the daughter of the architect, Frank Lloyd Wright. These young women, about six altogether, were called collectively the "calves" ("not already cow," Gurdjieff said), and there are many references to them, singly and together, in the diaries.

The French groups had been frequent and regular visitors to the flat at 6, Colonels Renard, but the sudden great influx of

English and Americans made changes necessary, as the little flat became impossibly overcrowded. At about the time of my arrival in 1949, it was arranged that the French groups should come for dinner only twice a week. On the French nights, the conversation was almost entirely French, and the Director also -Monsieur Bernard Lemaître. On French nights, we English kept out of the way.

Gurdjieff was truly hospitable and took great trouble, even when he was very ill, to see that his visitors were given the most considerate treatment. Part of the entertainment offered to them after the meals was provided by his music. He played one of those little hand organs so popular in the Near East: the instrument placed on his knees, one hand for the keyboard and the other working the bellows. On this he performed the most moving and unearthly music, which he varied to suit every occasion. When he was too tired or ill to play, we could listen to a recording.

One small point worth mentioning is that Gurdjieff could not - or did not - pronounce the letter H in the English way, but used G instead, as in the Russian. Thus "behind" became "begind" and "Mahomet" was "Magomet." On the other hand, "camel" for Gurdjieff became "hamel." It must be remembered also that in 1949 none of the Gurdjieff books was published. 'In Search of the Miraculous' was not published in England until 1950. Listening to the twice-daily readings was a privilege that we really appreciated. Typing the various manuscripts was also a task much sought after, and there were always plenty of volunteers.

I would like to say one more thing. Those readers who knew J.G. Bennett in the last twenty years of his life will be surprised by the picture of him in 1949 emerging from his own writings in this, his private diary. So certain that he knew how to work, so blind to the opportunities in front of him, so humorless, so determined that force - physical, mental, and moral - would bring him to the gates of heaven! In that month of August, 1949, he was obsessed with himself and his own subjective states, to the point of distorting Gurdjieff's instructions so

FOREWORD

that they would fit his own preconceived picture of what was needed to bring about liberation. Nevertheless, that month was the turning-point for him. His tolerance, humility and love - his deep understanding - so plain to see at the end of his life, first began to emerge during the visit to Gurdjieff recorded in this book. Those of us, so many of us, who benefited from his later teachings should thank not only J.G. Bennett, but above all his teacher, Gurdjieff.

I have added nothing to the text, but I have cut out one or two passages too personal to be of interest to anyone but the writer, and one or two details of Gurdjieff's illness and treatment. Apart from these small deletions, the manuscript is untouched.

Elizabeth Bennett, 1980

Diaries of J. G. Bennett and Elizabeth Bennett, 1949

J.G.B. Having in mind that I would be with Gurdjieff in Paris for a month, I decided to try to keep a record of my experience. By chance this book came into my hands.

July 23rd, 1949

J.G.B. COOMBE SPRINGS Last night I completed thirty hours' fast. As always, I am troubled by difficulty with attention and memory. Also I have to struggle very hard not to let other people see that I am in an irritable state. Yesterday I did not succeed at all well in this!

In the morning I had three phone calls to Paris. Mme. de Salzmann entirely approved and even praised my address to the Montessori Congress. I have now sent off a copy.

I gather that Gurdjieff did not say up to Thursday evening whether he was going to Geneva today, but I expect he will.

In the evening, I read the Katha Upanishad to the people who were here for dinner. It is noteworthy to observe the change in my feelings about the Katha. I always thought it one of the most noble poems in the world's literature and I admired above all the force with which the second and third Vallis strike the centre. But last night for the first time, it was concrete. I constantly felt, 'Yes, that is true and that is how it can and must be'.

I went to bed early, at midnight, and did not waken till nearly six-thirty, so I had an unusually good sleep and feel very much refreshed.

This morning I spent an hour on my knees in the Spring House. After forty minutes, I found I had the power to reach the Collected State. Afterwards the pain in my legs became too insistent. But once again towards the end, I began to sense my existence differently. I am not sure that I am doing it rightly, so I hope I shall have a chance of asking.

July 25th, 1949

    E.B. PARIS We all met at the café at 9.30. Mr. G. was already there, smoking, drinking tea and looking at us all without saying much. When his car came round he drove away and returned a few minutes later with his straw hat changed for his red fez.

    There were 3 cars, 5 people in each, and luggage on the roofs. We left Paris at 10. It was already hot, and the ends of the street were blurred and hazy. After driving for about one and a half hours we stopped by some trees for coffee, but only for a minute or two. At about 2 o'clock we stopped for a picnic lunch, somewhere beyond Sens. We spread out coats and sat beside the road: there was a thick hedge and tall trees, and it was very hot and dusty. The toasts were drunk in Armagnac; Marianne Director. (All the calves were very thirsty, but there was nothing to drink but Armagnac.) We ate kvoorma, brioches, goat cheese and melon, and of course much candy - we had brought a whole suitcase full of candy. When the bottle was empty, Gabo put it on the top of a high post by the road, and Mr. G. laughed and said that after the publication of "first série, my writing", anyone seeing such a thing would say, "Mr. Gurdjieff passed this way". He gave us - the young ones - no peace during the meal, shouting at us for not fetching things, for not eating, for eating too much, for not drinking honourably, for our idiocy in general, but when we had finished eating we sat quietly on the bank while he smoked. Mme. de Salzmann said that he had not seen Mme. Stjernval for 15 years, and how interesting tomorrow's meeting would be. She began to tell amusing stories of Mischa and Nikolai - how they "missed school together", how they went to America and made friends with Irish police in New York and "did not went to school". She was very amusing and very gay, and we all laughed and relaxed.

    We went on our way again, but after about half an hour we stopped beside a canal while Mr. G. slept for a couple of hours, as he usually does. Some of the others also slept, some swam in the canal. I went on to the town with Mme. de S., Mrs. Pearce, Eve and Sophia, to get Mrs. P.'s car attended to: it was getting too hot and inclined to boil over. I had hoped for a chance to speak to Mme. de S. and I was able to, while Mrs. P. was at the garage and the two girls in a café ordering drinks. Mme. de S. and I sat at a table on the pavement in the shade. It was by then very hot. The delay was long, because Mr. G. also had trouble with his car and stopped for some time at a garage.

The journey to Dijon was uneventful. We stayed at the Cloche d'Or.

The hotel was said to be full and people were being turned away, but Mme. de S. somehow ordered, and was given, 15 rooms! We had dinner in the restaurant at 10.30, at three round tables. I, by great luck, was beside Mr. G., on his right, and was able to look after him, pass things, change his plates, remind him to pass things, pour the drinks, etc. The others at the table were Mme. de S., Mrs. P., Mme. Godet, Mme. Caruso, Miss Anderson and Gabo. Mr. G. was undoubtedly very tired and hardly spoke, except a few remarks in Russian to Mme. de S. and Gabo. He gave the toasts himself, until he got bored with it and told Mrs. P. to do it. He told me that he was very tired. Yes, I said, it was too far to drive in such heat, and he nodded and said yes, and also all day *gaz* was very bad, but now he had taken his medicaments and was better.

After dinner five of us drank coffee in his room. The others went to bed. As soon as I had drunk my coffee and eaten the sweets he gave me I left, and I hope the others did too, so that he could go to bed.

July 26th

E.B. GENEVA We left Dijon at about 9. The usual order - Mr. G.'s car leading, Mme. Caruso's car second, Mrs. P. 'begind'. N. and I were with Mrs. P., also Eve and her brother, Paul. Mr. G. had been out early to buy Cassis. It was very hot.

We had planned to go into Switzerland by the Col des Faucilles, but as soon as we began to climb Mrs. P.'s car boiled over, not once but repeatedly, so we were soon left behind and took the other route, less mountainous. We lunched at Les Rousses, and enjoyed our day, though of course we were sad about getting separated from Mr. G. The final disaster was a tire burst, near Coppet, between Nyon and Geneva. We arrived at about 6.30 and found the others already installed. The hotels would not stay open so late, so we dined in the station buffet - very palatial, and quite unlike Liverpool Street!

It was an extraordinary meal - the table was very wide, and I personally could not even see Mr. G., let alone hear him, as he was at the far end on the same side as I, and I was at the bottom with the other Calves. So most of my account of the meal is at second hand. Dr. & Mrs. Egg were there, and Mme. Stjernval and Nikolai; also Russell Page, who joined us at Geneva and returned with us to Paris. There was an orchestra playing loudly quite near us, which made it impossible to hear Mr. G., and after a time he called the head waiter and gave him a large tip to stop the music. Anyway, he said, it was not music, but masturbation, and all the musicians were masturbators. The head waiter, probably expecting a compliment to the orchestra, said he did not understand this word - what did it mean? So Page was told to take the head waiter aside and explain to him the meaning, which he did. Marianne, who told me the story, said "Think of it, an old man like that, and he didn't know what masturbation was!" Her only reaction.

After dinner Gurdjieff went off for coffee with all the 'esteemed persons' and N., Marianne and I strolled back together to the hotel. When Marianne had arranged for his thermos to be filled for the night and seen that his room was ready, we went to bed.

July 27th

J.G.B. COOMBE SPRINGS On Monday night, I gave the last lecture of the series 'Introduction to the Ideas of G. I. Gurdjieff'. I chose 'Form and Sequence' as the chapter to read. I did not lecture very well - or rather I did not come to what I wanted to say.

Early on Monday morning as I was doing my inner task, I had the first glimpse of what it could be for 'non-desires to predominate over desires'. I have always thought that was an impossible state for me. I could not even contemplate trying to achieve it - certainly not wanting to. And I could see that, however painful it might be, the 'liberation from desires' which is so constantly taught in the Upanishads and Buddhist literature, is in fact necessary for the real self to be in command. Only I cannot bear the thought that I should cease to want certain human relationships. To be able to renounce them is one thing - not to want them seems to be the death of something precious in oneself.

And it may be that first that 'something' must die!

Last night I did the movements after a really hard day with H. and F. Three board meetings and long and difficult discussions.[1]

This morning I did my task very badly. How dreadful is this realization that 'I am taxi'!

E.B. CHAMONIX We spent the morning shopping and seeing the town. We left Geneva at 12.30. We should have left at 12, but we were half an hour late because Tanya was being sick. Mr. G. was annoyed at the delay and as a result shot away from the kerb without giving any directions as to where we were going. N. and I were with Mme. Caruso this time, Miss Anderson and Eve. We lost him before we left the town, but when we crossed the frontier at St. Julien we saw Mrs. P.'s car ahead, just passing through. We went to Annecy, but as

N. rather tartly pointed out, we did not come on the Trip to see Annecy; we came to see Mr. G., and in this we were not being successful.

By this time, we had given up all pretense of pursuit and went on at our own pace - a wonderful drive over the mountains. About 10 kilometres outside Chamonix we came round a sharp corner and there was Mrs. P.'s car, with Paul's legs sticking out from under it. A group of disconsolate Calves was standing near, and on the opposite side of the road, on a pile of stones, very upright and perfectly composed, sat Mme. de Salzmann. Apparently they had driven over a large rock and

---

[1] At that time J.G.B was a Director of Powell, Duffryn and Company.

damaged the undercarriage.

We waited till they were ready to go on, and then Mme. de S. came with us and we drove into Chamonix. Madame said, "This road remembers the Caucasus", pronouncing it 'Cowcasus'.

Mr. G. was already resting when we arrived, so we settled into our rooms, looking straight on to Mont Blanc and Mont Maudit, with the perpetual roar of the glacier stream in our ears. N. and I went for a walk and listened to the cow bells.

At dinner Mr. G. sat at the head of the table with Gabo beside him.

Then on each side came Mme. de S., Mrs. P., Page, Marianne, Mme. Caruso, Miss Anderson, Mme. Godet and then N. and me: once more we could not hear. But we saw. He was tired, and Gabo was very good, being a clown and making him laugh. He said tomorrow we must have '*salade*', and told Gabo to find a suitable receptacle. Gabo brought a huge aluminium pot from the kitchen, which was rejected with scorn, and finally Mr. G. agreed to use a large flower vase. Then there was the comedy of the actual mixing of the *salade*, which took a long time and was very funny to watch. At the end of the meal I asked Page if I had missed any Cosmic Truths, and Page said, no, there were none: only comedy. To bed early, all of us tired.

July 28th

E.B. CHAMONIX We spent the whole day at Chamonix. At lunch I abandoned all attempts to hear what Mr. G. said, and sat opposite him at the far end of the long table, so that though I could not listen, I could look. I did hear one thing, though; he spoke again about Enlightened Idiots and their terrible position, unable to go forward because of their heredity.

After lunch we moved to the other room for coffee. I sat beside him and took his tarboosh and his stick, etc. Mrs. Egg was feeling overcome by the heat, and getting greener and greener. He put a cigarette in its holder and fumbled in his pocket, as I thought, for matches, so I produced matches myself. But he did not want that: he was looking for pills for

JULY 28TH

Mrs. Egg, which he gave her, and she began to look better. Then he began really to search for matches, so I struck one, and lit his cigarette. He said, "Ah, Yelizabet, you are very kind. First time, I not understand". I said that I also did not understand the first time. "Then you can enter into my feelings. For this I will give *cadeau*", and he gave me two chocolates filled with Benedictine.

A young woman, a nursemaid, passed with a small child in her arms; a dark little boy of about 3 years old. Mr. G. called her to him and gave her sweets, some for her and some for the child. She stayed for a minute or two and then, as she moved away, asked him who he was: was he an Egyptian? He smiled and said no, he was "universal". Then, pulling down the ends of his mous*tâche* - "sometimes I am Chinese, and sometimes" - turning the mous*tâche* up and holding the ends out stiffly - "I am Italian". We all laughed and the nursemaid moved away, but as she went out of sight to her place behind the piano and a large vase of flowers, the baby protested and began to cry. Mr. G: smiled. "You see? He not wish leave me", and got out another handful of sweets. Sophie jumped up to take them to the child, and he sent instructions about giving some of the sweets now and some at night, in bed. "Now", he said, "hear him *rit*". For a moment there was silence, and then the child did indeed laugh, and Mr. G. was much pleased.

We spent the evening swimming, walking to the foot of the glacier, etc., and dined as usual at about 10.30. I was nearer to Mr. G. tonight, and able to hear quite a lot of what went on. He teased Iovanna about her habit of disappearing to the tops of mountains just when she was needed, etc., and said how she is always active, and how she is a "monstrosity" and should be in a circus: he would build a cage for her, "big, big", because she must have room to move about, and she must give him nine per cent of her earnings.

He told Tanya that he had said many things useful for her, but she could not listen or understand: this was not her fault, but her heredity - "such grandmother have". He told a rude story about a substitute for castor oil and he asked me if I knew what onanism is. When I said, all wide-eyed, "No, please tell me", he said it was the same as masturbation. This was à propos Shakespeare, who was "not onanist, but passive pederast", and how "such dirty thing" had ruined the British language as Pushkin had ruined the Russian.

At the end of the meal, when we were all more or less overfed, he offered 2,000 francs to whoever would eat a certain bowl of iced raspberries and cream. Sophie took it and divided it with three others; they each got 500 francs. Then he said the dining room was not cozy, we would go outside for coffee, where we could continue our 'cozy chat'. Before he went he held up his half-eaten segment of melon and said who could clean this so that it could be painted - tomorrow he wished to paint this skin and give it as a present to a friend - who would prepare it for him? Paul said he would, and Mr. G. said Eve could help him and if they did it properly he could have 1,000 francs. When we left the dining room Eve and Paul were sitting at the table still, with their heads together over the melon skin.

Over coffee Mr. G. was unusually talkative. He talked, in rather an obscure way, so that probably those who did not know the story would not understand, about his recent cure of Mme. C.'s back, and how she had not yet paid for this. Not with money - she had certainly paid with money, but that was not enough; she must pay with work. He turned to Mme. Godet and said see how she does not listen, she is dreaming. Dreaming about her family, wondering about her children, gaining nothing by this and also losing what is going on round her. When he had invited her to go on the trip, he said, she had said yes without thinking of the children: now the trip was going on longer than she had expected, but it was too late. She should not be here: she should be with her children, who were young, and needed her. How could she tell what would happen to them in her absence: they might become" "masturbators, or like father". When he invited her she should have said she could not leave her children, and then perhaps he could have arranged something: he loved children and would have been glad to have them on the trip.

At this point Paul came back with his melon skin and showed it to Mr. G. They bent over it together, very solemn, and then G. said, no, it wasn't quite good enough: nothing yellow should remain. Paul went solemnly off to fetch a razor blade and Mr. G., watching him go, laughed and said, "See now what education he have". Until now he knew nothing, he only knew how to eat and shit, "never he work with this", tapping his forehead, "now this his first *labeur*". When Paul came back again after an interval, the skin was perfect: Mr. G. folded it and put it in his pocket and gave the 1,000 francs - "not forget sister".

Then he took up the glass of Perrier he was drinking with his coffee and said to Marianne, "Tell". She said, "To the health of all ordinary wise men". He was silent for a moment, and then said, "Truth, this very old science, science Idiotism", and went on to say that it was 4,500 years old, older than Babylon, and how it should only be used by "initiate persons". When he had learnt it, (I *thought* he said in Tibet, but I can't be certain), he had decided to make use of it to teach people, though really it was not his to use, and for this the initiate persons did not like him. But in the new world it would be used. Because he is going to make war on the old world: he is going to break our so-called God, with the long beard and the comb in his vest pocket. Then everyone who wishes to learn must read again and again "first *série* my writing". Those who want to understand more must study the second series, and those who want being must study the third series. But this would be very expensive; it would cost either 5 *zéros*, English, or very hard work. This is the first time I have heard him talk in this way about much work as an alternative to *zéros*. After this the party broke up and we all went to bed.

July 29th

E.B. VICHY This morning we left at 9.30 for Vichy. Mr. G. sat on a bench by the front door and watched us running to and fro loading the cars. N. managed to get into Mr. G.'s car today, because Marianne was afraid of being sick: she travelled in the back of Mme. Caruso's car with Page and me.

We had lunch at Nantua. By the lake: it looked lovely. Afterwards we drove on for some way and then stopped by the road for Mr. G. to rest.

Usually he stops for at least an hour and, counting on this, Paul and Tanya wandered off. When Mr. G. wanted to go on, 20 minutes later, they were not to be found, and though we all blew our horns they did not come. So Sophie moved into our car and Marianne went in Mme. Caruso's. Mr. G.'s car and Mrs. Pearce's went on, leaving Mme. Caruso's car behind to wait for Paul and Tanya, her car being the fastest and best able to catch up. (In fact they never did catch up, but went to Vichy by a more direct route than ours, and were already at the Hotel Albert Premier when we arrived.) So we went: in G.'s car, besides himself, Gabo, N., Mme. Godet and Iovanna, and in Mrs. P.'s car, Sophie, Eve, Page and me.

We got hopelessly lost. He began to aim for Lyon and Clermont Ferrand, and then turned off before we reached either and went north again, on by-roads. Apparently Gabo couldn't read the map, and Mme. Godet thought she could, but read it all wrong. N. was saying nothing and Iovanna was asleep. When we, behind, at last realized they were lost, we pulled up beside them at every cross road, and told them which way. Once we stopped for a rest by the road and once, at dusk, we stopped for water at a café. (It was, incidentally, a wonderful day's driving: the Mont Blanc massif, the Haute Savoie and the Jura - lovely to look at).

We arrived at last at Vichy. It seemed months since we were there.

We had dinner again in the private dining room, and again he called the manager to drink with us and made a fool of him. He paid little attention to anyone else. I was fascinated to see how the manager was entirely helpless, not knowing he was being played with, reacting unconsciously. When the man was quite drunk, Mr. G. said something about how, when we saw him being polite to someone, we must also behave in the same way, especially now, where the manager was an important person, whereas he, Mr. G., was "small man".

The meal did not go on long: we were all tired, and went at once to bed.

July 30th

 E.B. PARIS We left at 9.30 for Paris. Mr. G. sat at a small table at the door, drinking Perrier and watching us load the cars. After his experience yesterday, when his passengers were no use to him, he announced that he would have only men in the car besides Marianne. As, at the same time, he would not take Paul with him, this wasn't possible, so I cautiously edged my way in. He was not particularly pleased to see me, and said not was place here, but Marianne said briskly, yes, there was, and he said no more. So Gabo went with him in front and I sat at the back, hardly daring to breathe, between Marianne and Page. As time went on, however, when he found that we were not going to give trouble, he became increasingly amiable, and we relaxed.

 We drove fast, and did not stop till we were beyond La Charité, where he left the car by the road and got out for a few minutes' rest.

 He sat on a pile of stones, with his back against a tree, the sky and the river bright blue behind him; the sand and the scorched string-coloured grass were shimmering with the heat. He was in a patch of deep shade, sitting with his leg tucked under him and his other leg stretched out, his hands on his knees. He wore his fez and a cream-coloured suit, paler than his face. He sat smoking and smiling at us all as we sat round him, saying little.

 He said how fast we had come, as if we had been flying, and that his tape-worm was beginning to create *scandale*.[1] There was a discussion about the monastery at La Charité. We were there about 20 minutes, I suppose, and then we went on into Pouilly for lunch.

 Lunch proceeded amiably enough until, at the end, we all began to order fruit, ices, etc. He said, we need not wait here,

---

1 Meaning that he was hungry.

we will go on and drink coffee later, and eat dessert. But some of us still persisted, asking the waitress for peaches, grapes and what not, and then he let fly.

Why did we go on ordering food when he had told us it was not necessary? "You not think who pay - you think Muchransky[1] pay, but no", it is he, Mr. G., who pays. "All the time I have seen - you think, because I am kind, he not notice, but now it is the last day." He has seen again and again how we order *orange pressé* when tea or coffee is there already: we order what we like, unnecessary things, and he has to pay. We think only of eating. Always until now he has put up with it, but never again. If, on the other hand, we work at this, pay attention and try to save him expense, treat it as a task, then perhaps we may still have a chance to be useful to him, and not die like dogs.

We trooped out to the cars and started on our way, but at Montargis we stopped at his usual café and drank Perrier with *citron*. He told everyone to "order what wish", and ordered ices for us all ... We had come fast, he said, and he was pleased. We stopped again just beyond Fontainebleau while he slept for three quarters of an hour, and then on to Paris, where we arrived at about 6.30.

It was an extraordinary trip - each one is always different from the others - I saw him less than on any other trip, and yet when I did see him I felt a great closeness to him.

We went back to the flat at 10.30 for dinner. We read 'Fragments'. There was a large crowd there: the Woltons, with two children, Dr. Walker, the two Jaloustres, Véra Daumal, Hylda, Bryn and Lucien, Dr. Bell and Miss Crowdie, Mr. Stewart, some English whom I don't know and various members of the French group, besides those sixteen who had been on the trip.

I could not get into the dining room, and have not been able to get a coherent account of the proceedings from anyone.

July 31st

J.G.B. COOMBE SPRINGS The 'Short Seminar' is going

---

[1] The legendary Georgian prince.

JULY 31ST

well. There are 41 people.

We started at 8 p.m. on Friday and finish at 8 p.m. on Monday. The plan is to read the whole of Beelzebub. So far we have finished Book 2 in about 24 hours actual reading time.

We do a 6-hour cycle - 4 hours reading, 2 hours for eating, sleeping, etc. Of the two hours, half an hour is given to Movements.

On the whole everyone is standing up to it very well. I have read so far - I do not know if my voice will hold out.

I rang up Paris this morning and spoke to Bryn, Elizabeth and Hylda. The trip appears to have been a great success.

Several things have become clearer to me from this complete concentrated re-reading of Beelzebub. I had not previously noticed the definite assertion that the 3 bodies correspond to the 3 foods. And the connection of 3rd body with Exioëhary.

Am I getting to the goal? I can see easily enough that I have a power over my body that 12 months ago I would not have believed possible. Also that I am free from much weakness in dealing with people. And I can make myself do what I decide.

But I have no more power over my attention than a year ago. *Less* than 20 years ago.

E.B. PARIS At lunch most of the conversation centred on S.W. She is a nice, intelligent, well-mannered child of 13 or 14. G. passed her some cream in a small bowl and she at once shared it with her brother. A few minutes later he said to her, "Not forget brother; *partagez*", and when he heard that she had already done so he was very pleased, and gave her some mango as a reward. Then he began a long talk with W. who, as Director, was sitting next to him, in a low voice, so that I, sitting in the fireplace, could hear very little. But he did say that if W. carried out his responsibilities towards her, she would be "wife of governor". I took this to be what he used to say to M.S., that she was 'candidate for wife of governor' when the new world was built.

In the evening he listened with great enjoyment to the

reading of 'Fragments', leaning forward with his elbow on his knee and his cigarette-holder in his hand, his eyes snapping, shaking with laughter at the references to himself.

At dinner he gave a wonderful dissertation on the education and conditioning of children. He began by giving sweets to Mrs. E. for her child. He said she should give them to him one at a time, and the first time say that it came from the man with the mous*tâche*, and "make like this" (he twirled the ends of his mous*tâche*). The second time she was to say that the sweet came from Mr. Gurdjieff, and again "make such". After that the child would be accustomed, and she need no longer say his name or make the mous*tâche* gesture. Then when the child came again to the flat, he would know Mr. G. as the man who sent him the sweets.

Turning to the table in general, he went on to talk about education, and danger, and fear. If a child has been properly educated and he finds a snake in his path, he will know what to do: he will grasp the snake *here* (with a gesture of closing his fist) so that the snake cannot harm him. The child is only a baby, and "not force have" to kill the snake, but he can hold it thus and "*cri*" and some older person will come (wonderful pantomime of attentive care in taking the snake from the child, removing it to a distance, and killing it). On the other hand, if the child has not been properly educated, he will find a snake in his path and not know what to do: he will be afraid, and become victim.

This was a long talk, and one of those quite impossible to reproduce. His gestures and expression and the variations of his voice were as important as the words. He acted it all - the first child grasping the snake but without strength to kill it, the arrival of the grown-up person, the panic and terror of the uneducated child. The audience also was attentive and perfectly silent.

The trip has been very good for him and he has scarcely coughed at all the last few days. I have never heard him cough so little at any time.

August 1st

E.B. We were very few at lunch today, because Mr. G. had spent the morning at the new place he has bought for his sister beyond Fontainebleau, and a rumour had gone round that he would not come back for lunch. In fact, he returned just before three, and we had lunch soon after. Sophie and I had been reading in turns.

Marianne had not come, so I was Director. This was the fourth time I have gone through the motions of being Director and the first time I have been able to relax and enjoy myself. This time I did not forget his 'plate' or forget what people were drinking (Norman was Verseur, and not very practised): I did not waste time in thinking how much better Mr. B. would have done it and let the Idiots come at their proper time and place, without frantic inner rehearsal beforehand. This was as well, because Mr. G. made me say Round Idiots and Zigzag Idiots, with full details, in French, and if I had been rehearsing this would have thrown me. The first time I was Director he made everything easy, the second time he made everything difficult; this time he left me to it.

It was very hot and oppressive and we all had headaches, more or less, and he felt the heat very much. He talked almost entirely about his sister's '*château*' and how he had taken the two architects, Adie and Entwhistle, with him this morning because it was "necessary *escalier* - go up chic - up-house" - in other words, it needs a new staircase to the loft, or attics. He spoke to me about my mispronunciation of Iovanna's name, and how it was correctly 'Yorgana', and my pronunciation was a *merdité* fostered and spread by the Roman Catholic Church. He talked about the difference between Japanese and Persian rice, and the desirability of eating yoghourt with both.

He spoke seriously to L., who had to leave early for the train for London. He said he must come back, if only for 3 hours: 3 hours all that was necessary. Why couldn't he come next week-end? Perhaps not enough oof? and various other things, only for L. When L. had gone, he said, "He very *naïf*, he thinks he can see Mr. G. for nothing, without work.

But I missed much of the conversation: I am not skilled enough as Director to be able to attend properly to him and do my duties as well.

Tonight was 'French night'. We met at the flat at 8.30 and the English reading was in Lise's room this time. Marianne read. The atmosphere was almost unbearable, and Mr. G. is not liking the heat. He came and sat with us for a few minutes, and almost fell asleep.

Dinner was at 10.45. The room was too full for me to get in, so I went and washed up in the kitchen. But I came in and out once or twice with plates, and once, during a lull in the kitchen, I sat on a little stool just inside the dining room door, so I was able to hear a few things. He talked very much in Russian tonight to Mme. de S.; I gathered he was telling her about his sister's *château*, but after that I could not understand.

He told Marianne that Lemaître was a real Director, whereas she was only *'candidat'*. She must watch Lemaître if she wanted to learn, and copy everything he does.

Once when I came in he was talking about divorce. I did not hear much, but he was saying that the English "marry, divorce, marry, divorce - in this way possible try every typicality". He told the story of the 'old Jewish galosh'. Page suggested 'cheesy' as a good description of the smell when the old Jew removed his galoshes before entering the synagogue, after wearing them for a week - "day, night, sleeping, waking, in bed ... ". At first G. did not like 'cheesy', but then he said after all not bad thing, because cheese also walks - that is how he likes his cheese. You take a piece of Roquefort, put on table, turn your back. When you turn round, Roquefort gone away. Pantomime of hunting about for the Roquefort. I heard much laughter during the evening.

The music tonight was extraordinary - wonderful. I have never heard him play in that way before.

August 2nd

J.G.B. COOMBE SPRINGS The effort of attention for the reading was sometimes almost beyond my power. Several times I found myself saying things that were quite unconnected with the reading. Once I threw out my arm and pointed to a non-existent *étagère* in the middle of the room. My chief physical trouble was that my tongue got swollen and I had to keep drinking cold water to prevent it from being cut by my teeth. I had practically no difficulty with my larynx. But for the most part I read well enough.

The people struggled really hard. We all worked together on Saturday for 4 hours. In the evening on Monday we had a really good Feast. I made a pilaf with Persian rice that Gurdjieff gave me. Persian rice cooked in 2½ lbs. of butter and 3 pints of milk. Then added 54 eggs whipped up. Stirred it all till it was just setting. A most noble dish. We also had entrecote minute for which I cut 42 steaks from the big joint. We started with 'salade' - a good imitation of the Paris *salade*, only not quite strong enough! We finished with melon. Afterwards I drove H. and C.M. back to London. By 6.30 I was awake, very fresh and well. Visited the spring and had a good 35 minutes of contemplation.

E.B. PARIS Lunch today was very interesting. Marthe did not come, so I did her job, standing by the piano and serving. W. was Director and when he drank his wife's health at the appropriate Idiot, Mr. G. took much interest in it and said the fact that W. remembered showed that they could not have been married long; after one year he would already be thinking only about divorce, like the other English and Americans. I was pleased that this had come up again, after the snatch I heard last night. He went on to say that the English and Americans marry and divorce many times, so that in the end it comes to the same thing as a *bordel*. When we marry, we take an oath before God. But the fact that we can so readily break our oath before God showed how little we value God - we spit on our God. In any case, he said, masturbation had spoilt English family life - all the English are masturbators.

He told Sophia that until Tanya returns she is to be official 'Egout pour Sweet' and Sophia took the little bowl from him. He 'introduced' M.P. to Marianne, and explained how Marianne was one of the six girls he had brought with him from America, so that he could teach them, and when they went back they could make a thousand people happy. "But they not use me": they might perhaps make five people happy, but as far as he was concerned they could go to the devil. This loses much in writing: when he spoke it was terrifying. He spoke very quietly.

In the evening he was enjoying the reading from 'Fragments' so much - Chapter XII, about the right use of sex energy - that we did not start dinner till ten to twelve. I sat in my corner by the piano, and the conversation was almost entirely about his sister's *château*, the new drawings, the plans for its organization, etc. He did not eat much: he said that although it was so late he wasn't hungry.

August 3rd

E.B. When we reached Hopeless Idiots at lunch, Mr. G. told me to give the Addition. We drank, and went on eating. And then he turned to me again (I was almost opposite him, Bouche d'Egout) and said there is another Addition, but only leaders of groups, etc. know it. This says that in order to die honourably one must work *now*: if not work *now*, it is all masturbation, imagination. If we do not work now we will die, not only like dogs, but like very dirty dogs.

I thought a lot about this. I remembered the day last autumn when he linked Pierre and me as 'herrings out of the same barrel', with 'the same smell', and talked about the disease of tomorrow. Did he say to me at lunch, work *now*, don't wait till next Friday, or did he say, your work is imagination, start *now*? - I don't know.

M.P. is returning to England on Friday, so he told her that until she leaves she must eat double, and build up a reserve. Like the sheep with the fat tail, who lives on the fat in emergency. Or the camel, who "puts food some special place, not even digest", until it needs it. M. must do this. In fact, the sheep and 'hamel' are better than man; man, who should be like God, has to learn from the animals. Though he doesn't believe it, because

AUGUST 3RD

he thinks himself very great. In reality, man is like louse; both unimportant things, both easy to destroy.

Lonya[1] arrived today from America.

Mary S.[2] he told us, wrote asking him, if he saw a "very extraordinary cat", to send it to her. "And truth, one such I see", while he was on the trip last week. So he told me to pack it up and send it to her.

He fell asleep over the music, so we all left quickly when the first piece was over.

B. left at 9.30 for London. H. and I went to St. Lazare to see her off. When we came to the flat tonight Gabo was hanging pictures in the reading room, directed by Mr. G. There were pictures in moulded frames stacked against the chairs and all over the bed: we had to clear them all away before we could sit down. Gabo went to do more picture-hanging in the dining room, and Page began to read Chapter XIII of 'Fragments'. It is not surprising that the music recordings are so bad these days: with all those pictures and all those people I am surprised it works at all. It was difficult to concentrate on the reading tonight; the room was hot and stuffy and overcrowded; people came late, climbing to their places over other people, Mme. de S. called me out to speak to me, Gabo hammered in the next room. We went on till midnight, when we started dinner.

Gurdjieff did not begin to eat for a very long time. Sometimes he says he makes such a long preparation - composing a *salade*, etc. - in order to give himself an appetite when he is not hungry: perhaps this was so tonight. Anyway, for a long time he prepared his *salade* and hors d'oeuvres without speaking. In fact, throughout the meal he spoke very little. He got slower and slower as time went on, and at the end was very sleepy. We did not help him: I thought Russell Page was the only one who was any use. The Director was so sleepy that he was actually swaying in his chair, and did not change Mr. G.'s plates without repeated whispered reminders. Mrs. P. did not get up from the table till 2 a.m., and H. and I felt absolutely doped with sleep for about the last hour - I don't know what

1 Lonya Savitsky, Tanya's brother
2 Aged 7

happened to us all. H. and I were on either side of Mrs. P.

He talked again about the *château*, and how the *escalier* was to be made of - "Marble?" said Entwhistle. "No, mosaic", said Page, "Blue, white and black; one step blue, one white and the next black". Mr. G. said he must finish the arrangements because he wanted to go in a day or two to Tibet. "Tibet, Monsieur?" said Page. "Or Dieppe?" Mr. G. gave him a perfectly wicked and sly smile and said, "Either very expensive", as though apart from that the destination did not matter much. Then he began to say how in the *château* a lamp would burn, using the same oil "what use Jerusalem, Christ's Temple", and went on to say that he is one of the four 'Commanders of the Knights of the Holy Sepulcher, and have special order'. Page said, "I bet you wear it the wrong way round", and he laughed and said, yes, he never forget his grandmother.[1]

He said how the head of this Order came and spent several weeks at the Prieuré, and used to go to the highest part of the Russian bath there. "He very big valise[2] have: this very comic thing - everybody wish laugh, but only *intérieurement* - he not tail of donkey." And how later this man died in his sleep - "In evening, lie on bed, sleep. In morning, not wake up - die". And, "Truth, he deserve such die, without suffering - he very good man".

We left at 2.30.

August 4th

E.B. Marianne told me that she is able to understand now his sudden refusal to let her go to England, when he had first encouraged her to go. She said she had not only learnt from this that she has no strength to carry out a resolution, but also, by his constant harrying on the trip, he has made it possible for her to pass a barrier, which in any case she must pass at some time or other, and which, by going to England, she would only have postponed.

I forgot to say something about yesterday: he said to W. at dinner that he had put W. in charge of the publication in

1   A reference to an instruction in 'All and Everything'.
2   Stomach.

England of *Belzébuth* - a year ago he had told him to hurry. And now, when he asks, he finds nothing has been done. This has caused great loss to Mr. G., etc., and he led the talk into a harangue against the English. Obviously all this was not to be taken literally, and he frequently turned to Mrs. W., saying, "You see?" or "Now you understand?".

He gave some very hot peppers to Marianne and Mrs. Pearce, and at the same time he was himself drinking some Calvados which pleased him very much. He said it was "*feu concentré*", and as it went down inside him he held up his finger and seemed to listen, then nodded in a satisfied way and said, "Everything make *chemin* with pleasure". Meanwhile, Mrs. P. had eaten her peppers without turning a hair, but Marianne, with an agonized expression and tears in her eyes, was coughing and eating bits of bread. He turned to her and said that this was wrong: if she suffered *intérieurement* she must never show this outside. "Look at Mrs. P.", he said. Besides, if one ate food the first time without any fuss (I forget the words, but he implied, if you show who is master), the second time it will be your friend. Like him with the Calvados, he added, raising his glass.

The soup was new at lunch, and Page, as Egout, suggested that Mr. G. should try it. He did so, and at once called Lise and told her she was an idiot for not putting into it more salt and more tomato. When she had gone, he smiled on us all and said how his interior calm is never disturbed. Sometimes it is necessary for him to manifest as he did to Lise, but when he does this it is for the good of the other person: he himself feels only pity for him, and is still tranquil *intérieurement*.

I learnt much from the trip last week. There was an interesting collection of people, some of them new: N., Paul, Mme. Godet, Mme. Caruso, Miss Anderson - and trips do show up people in an entirely new light. N., for instance; I have known her on and off for about 12 years, yet I learnt things about her on the trip that I had not known before.

This was 'French night', and Page began to read at 8.30. We finished all we had of 'Fragments' and went on to 'Impartial Mentation'. I was haunted by the inscription over the entrance to Purgatory in the chapter before, "Only he can enter here who puts himself in the position of the other results of my labours".

At dinner he told the stories of the Irish, Scotch and English for the benefit of Sophie Young, whose first visit was tonight, and when he called for 'Egout pour Sweet', Rina made a spectacular entrance, as from a trap-door. She and Pierre had just arrived.

I, in my corner, passed my soup to W., who had none; he in turn passed it to Dr. Egg, who also had none. All this went quite unnoticeably and without uproar, but I need hardly say that it did not escape Mr. G. Much later in the meal, he said, looking at our end of the table, "Everybody tasted soup?" and to me directly, "You tasted?"

"No, I didn't". He raised his eyes to heaven and shrugged his shoulders. Then, "I advise eat. This makes possible everything else digest. How possible you not eat? You see" - to Mme. de S. - "*extérieurement* she" (he made an expressive little gesture), "but *intérieurement* - phoo-phoo."

He has made a passing remark several times lately about the toast to all Squirming Idiots, and to the health of all hysterical women, and has gone on to say, how else can his ideas spread, than by hysterical people coming here and talking about it afterwards? And so on.

August 5th

J.G.B. On the way to France. I have tried to keep up as far as possible the intensity of effort during this week. Not more than 3 1/2 hours' sleep, exercise[1] several times a day, interference with normal habits.

It has been a hard week at the office. Reports to finish, reorganization plan for labs.

On Tuesday evening I was at home and spoke to several of the household individually. Finished at a quarter to one and then began work on the Pakistan report and the article for Colliery Engineering. Finished at 2.30 a.m. On Wednesday evening I had a serious talk with P. and tried to show him how

---

1   Inner or spiritual exercise.

terrible it is to think that God can be mocked. He had missed the seminar to go off on some private whim. How very sharp is his dual nature.

E.B. PARIS I have seen several things today most clearly from the behaviour of P. and R., and of Mr. and Mrs. B. on their arrival. The dreadful power and 'ingenuity' of slavery. It is strange that, of all of them who have helped me before, it should be P. this time who explained it all.

At lunch I did Marthe's job, but first we read 'Bogachevsky'. G. tried, with every sort of help, to make me invent an 'addition' to Round Idiots, but I was too stupid and could not do it.

W., as Director, said, 'Zigzag' when he should have said, 'Squirming', and was made there and then to change places with Marianne, who was Director for the rest of the meal.

I have been thinking today about Mr. G.'s power of building up an unbearable situation. He does, but then what can one do but bear it? Cheat, I suppose, calm oneself, drown it in sleep - I don't know.

August 6th

J.G.B. PARIS There are many things I want to write about the conversations, but I have no time yet. G.'s tactics towards me are fairly clear: he is keeping me at arm's length and preventing me from speaking to him about myself.

E.B. We read the first half of 'Heptaparaparshinokh' today. I was glad: I have never heard it all. It is very difficult to understand.

August 7th

J.G.B. We talked last night till 2.30. I woke up at 6.15 very tired and with head aching. I spent an hour doing my inner tasks. My heart beating very strongly and as if in a catalepsy, unable to move a limb. All the time I was sharply aware of my impotence. By what means could I hope to have an 'I'? I realized that nothing that I am doing now can possibly give *this* to me.

When I got up I felt full of doubt and uncertainty as to what I should do next. We had to go to the Bank of France to get petrol coupons and francs. Then to the movements practice with Alfred at the Entwhistles' house. We worked for about an hour on the Tibetan and on No. 32. I felt quite different after this and realized that as long as I can practice the movements every day I shall be all right here.

I brought Frick and a man from the Hague group to lunch. I do hope that Frick will join the work seriously. He and Mme. de Salzmann made a rendezvous before I left.

The special task I have set myself of aloofness from everyone I care for and friendliness to all those that are indifferent to me can produce a very strong effect.

We read the Introduction to the 3rd Series before lunch. I saw at once that this secret - of exteriorizing by abnegation of something which is precious to oneself and not harmful in its own nature - may be the only thing to create permanent self-remembering. The question is whether I am strong enough to do it persistently and consistently.

Three days ago, I swore an oath before my own essence that I would never let anything for the rest of my life come before the work for me. That means I must do what is best for the work wherever I see it. But of course, often I shall not see.

This morning I debated with myself whether to go to the café. I decided not to go. When I went to the flat to ask permission for Frick and Mulder, I felt an unmistakable reaction in Mr. G. He was cooking pilaff and I could tell that he was glad to see me, but quite prepared to jump on me about something.

On the whole, I have so often changed my own inner state that I cannot describe anything clear and definite.

E.B. Mr. G. spoke to me after lunch today, and all my 'private affairs' simply did not exist any more. I don't know what he did: he just talked to me about how badly he needed *zéros* - once before I helped him, etc. - and I stuck out and argued and said, "That is all right for you; you need help next week. What about me; I need help now, today", and so on.

The happening of last night is so shattering for me that I could not write about it then. Now I must say what happened to me at dinner last night.

No, it is no good. I can't write about what happened on Thursday night. I shall have to leave it.

August 8th

J.G.B. We have for two days read and re-read the Introduction to 3rd Series. This and other factors have made clear to me tonight how I must work. Then Mr. G. crystallized it all when he said to me at the end of the reading, "Not will sleep, but do the task I give you!"

The 3rd Series has one tremendous effect - of making efforts seem more necessary, more possible and at the same time of making what I do seem very puny and second-rate.

E.B. Yesterday at lunch G. talked about Buddha's *valise* being due to tripe. And when he talked about stupid English, Mr. B. said not when they have read 'Beelzebub', and when people can walk in the street and see who is dead and who is alive. G. gave the story - for Miss Virgo's benefit - of the English tourists climbing the hill, but with one addition - they have with them a Cook's guide book, "because Cook make *monde*".

Mrs. E. was sitting at the little side table, not able to see G., but she had her head turned back over her shoulder so that she could watch him in the strip of looking glass on the sideboard. When Mr. G. looked round and said, "Mrs. Mephisto not here?" Mr. B. said, yes, she was there in the corner, meditating. While she was explaining what she was really doing I thought how strange this is: Mr. B. and many of the other directors have never sat anywhere but in the Director's chair: they can't possibly know all the ins and outs of the room. That may be one reason why Marianne is a good Director - she knows.

There was some conversation about how he can tell easily, at some distance, by seeing a corpse, whether or not that person died honourably, but I did not hear it; I was in the kitchen. But on Sunday at lunch he spoke about it again, very briefly: how this (dying honourably) was a small aim, and it was possible to tell whether or not a person had achieved it, by looking at their corpse.

Today was interesting at lunch: the 'Notarius' was there, who had never been to a meal of Mr. G.'s before and knows nothing of his ideas; Mr. Frick, who equally had not been there before but knew of the ideas, and Mr. Mulder, from the Hague, in the same boat as Mr. Frick, but less well prepared. Myself, I thought the Notarius took the prize: he really listened when Mr. G. spoke - he was Egout, by the way - and he did not consider[1] in the least, and fell in with all the ceremonies and was very observant. Mr. Frick talked a lot at first, and twice talked all through a speech of Mr. G.'s, causing us all to lose it, but he became quiet towards the end and seemed to begin to listen. He makes Armagnac, with his own vineyards and what-not, and he had a very funny argument with Mr. G., who swore that Frick's Armagnac could not possibly be any good. He speaks Russian, too, which went well.

This evening was French night. We read in G.'s bedroom, the Prologue to the 3rd Series. G. was there when we finished it, and Mr. B. said, "What a wonderful chapter!" "Wonderful?" "Yes, what power!" Mr. G. nodded gravely. "Then not sleep so much", but work to read and understand and have such power oneself.

They have been rehanging all the pictures in the flat, and among other alterations they have hung a new curtain behind G.'s chair in the dining room. This is much better, as a curtain, than the other, but it is dark blue with clumps of red flowers arranged on it symmetrically, and this is a bad background for him. The old curtain was a rather unpleasant sort of rusty mustard colour, but it took the light very well and seemed to suit his dark face. In fact I have sometimes thought that the old hanging may in some way account for the curious appearance I have twice seen.

M. Lemaître was Director tonight, and Mr. B. Egout.

<u>G. told a new</u> story tonight - or rather, he used an allegory

1   Feel embarassed or self-conscious.

that I have not heard before. He said that when he returns from America he will settle down to cultivate his kitchen garden. First one must prepare the ground, then one must plant seeds, then one must keep it weeded and root out the useless vegetables, etc. And we must understand that he can do this more quickly than anyone: he can do in half an hour what other people would take long over. Then he passed to how Mme. de S. and Mr. B. knew what he could do in this direction - hadn't he built the Study House[1] in three days?

I didn't hear much, though; it was crowded and I was in and out all the time.

August 9th

J.G.B. If I do not make a daily programme with myself and stick to it, I shall find my stay here at least half ruined. I have so far only organized the early morning by rising at 6.30 to do one hour's inner exercise and then practice movements.

E.B. Mr. B. commented on how much more G. eats these days, and indeed since he returned from Geneva he has eaten extraordinarily much, for him.

I am refusing to listen to the voice that tells me that my task is too big for me. l must refuse to listen, because of all the tasks in the world this is the one that I must without fail fulfill 'honourably'. This has a special value because it is not even primarily my task. I say I *must* do it, but I haven't the least idea whether or not I *can*. But I must and will, so that's that. Mr. G. has an extraordinary way of compressing the situation, of removing one prop after another, until you are forced to see the bones.

After lunch today I said to him: "If I go with you to America, may I travel with you? On the same ship?" He nodded amiably. "Of course. But wait. I have another idea. All this" - he made a wide gesture with his hand, "many valuable thing is". He *gaz*ed affectionately at Cleopatra with her asp; at that woman with the pigeon biting her ear, and went on to say that

[1] Reference to the large hall, the Study House, built at the Prieuré in Avon when Gurdjieff's Institute was there.

when he went to America he could not leave these splendours unattended - would I stay and look after them, with Lise? Yes, of course I would, gladly. "Not go in America - next time". (This gave me a secret amusement; there has already been so much heart-burning over *this* visit, let us hope he won't begin to plan the next just yet!) "Live here", he added, driving the point home, and I said I would love to do it. "Thank you", he said. "And thank you what you understand so quickly. For this I make reward".

In the evening I spoke to him again as I was going away and said would he agree to give me a task "before you go away". I meant America, but he thought I meant the trip to Dieppe tomorrow. He said, "When say 'I', feel. When say 'am', sense. Even every hour". I nodded. "You not surprised what I make so few words?" And then, that if I will stay tomorrow and not go to Dieppe, he will reward me three times.

All this is very well, but I believe I have never lived through a day as difficult as this.

August 10th

J.G.B. For four days I have stumbled along in a state of bewilderment and uncertainty. Now I can see the nature of the two-fold task I have to accomplish. Through the help of Mme. de S., I have seen clearly the second task. Of course he could not tell me directly, since it consists in opposing his will. It is a task of very great importance for me. Whether I can accomplish it is still quite impossible to say. With the other task I expected suffering and struggle, but no actual inability to perform it at a given moment. But this task is precisely the opposite - there is no suffering or struggle - but merely the inability at a given moment to say 'No'!

E.B. Today Mr. G. was due to go to Dieppe. He said he would leave at 3, and consequently he cut short the reading almost before it was started and we began lunch at 1.45. Very few people. He talked about who was to travel with who and what the plans were, etc. Then Mme. de S. telephoned to say

AUGUST 10TH

she could not get rooms in Dieppe, so Mr. G. said, right, try Rouen. The answer to this was yes, there are rooms in Rouen. Then say, said Mr. Gurdjieff peacefully, that I not will go today after all. So, just like that, the trip was off, the cars unloaded and the suitcases unpacked.

Between lunch and dinner, Mr. B. drove us to Chartres. The after lunch music was wonderful.

Dinner was amusing, and Mr. G. certainly enjoyed himself. I forgot to say that we had the story of the French butter the other night, with the fruitiest bits at the end in Russian, which was just as well. And the story of Mullah Nassr Eddin riding his donkey when very drunk and wanting to know the time. And the entrancing story of how once an archangel asked God, "Your Endlessness, why you love who love parents?" to which God replied that he who loves his parents makes place which God Himself can enter.

In the evening Mme. de S. left early, before dinner was over, and Mr. B., who was Director, told me to drive her home, which was nice of him. I told her about Mr. G. telling me not to go to America, but to stay and guard the flat, and she said, why, she wondered. I said that in any case I should go ahead with the arrangements, and she agreed. "But don't disregard what he says about the flat: this means that here is someone he can trust. And," she said, "how do you feel about it? Do you wish to go?" "No, not really; only that I want to be with Mr. G." Yes, but also this was an interesting experience, to see him in new places, handling different situations.

She asked how long I have been here and said I must look on this as a time for storing up impressions and knowledge, for learning, not for putting into practice. Later, I shall find conditions when this knowledge will be necessary, but that is not now.

She went on to ask about my own personal affairs. I explained to her how I felt and in what way I had changed in this since I came, and she listened and nodded and did not comment.

I came back to the flat to find them playing a new recording, and I had a few words with Mr. G. before I left.

August 11th

E.B. At lunch Mr. B. tried to get Mr. Gurdjieff to talk about the Last Supper, but he wouldn't. He teased Mr. B. and wriggled out of it, saying that there were also hundreds of parasites there, etc. It all arose from his saying that the English don't know how to eat: they eat to live (he didn't use that phrase, but it is the best translation I can do), whereas they should eat with pleasure.

We ate delicious fish, and someone made a joke about being at Dieppe. He smiled and said, "yes; mountain come Magomet".

The other day, at the end of a meal, when Egout gave him a cigarette and Poubelle lit it for him, he said, "See now how my life is roses, roses. And I - only a poor old dancing teacher".

This was French night, and at the end of it C.M. fell over an obstruction in the passage and broke her arm.

August 12th

J.G.B. I am learning so much so fast that it is impossible to keep pace with it.

This evening has been extraordinary. It was French night. I read the Introduction to the 2nd Series and Material Questions in G.'s room. He came in at the end of M.Q. and everyone laughed heartily at the story of the 'workshop'. He enjoyed it too.

When we went in I pushed Lemaître forward as Director and when G. asked, "Who will be Director in next room?" I offered and he said, "Yes, will be good". It was the first time that I had not eaten close beside him and I could feel the general atmosphere.

I drove Mme. de S. home after dinner and spoke to her about *zéros*. I also said that I was receiving wonderful help for my own work, but if she were to ask me in what it consists, I could not say. She said, "This I understand *very* well".

I returned to the flat as G. was playing and knelt at the door. Afterwards he called me in to take a place opposite him.

AUGUST 12TH

Afterwards I went off with Lonya, Boussic, Marie-Claude and Marthe and we drank coffee at St. Germain. I returned here with Lonya at 2.30.

Today I have not rested at all and I only had 3 hours' sleep. But I was tired during the reading which lasted nearly two hours.

Lonya spoke to me about Mr. G.'s great respect for his grandmother, and showed that usual unswerving loyalty to her which is such a beautiful property of his.

E. told me of conversations with Marianne about U.S.A. and the peculiar state of exclusion and separation that exists there. Mrs. V. also spoke of it. She finds the 'austerity' at Mendham rather forbidding.

E.B. At lunch today I watched Mr. G. making his bowl of *salade*. This never loses its charm for me. I love to watch his gravity over the whole proceeding, the way he hunts about among the bottles in front of him for the exact sauce or condiment he needs. I love seeing him solemnly pour in the whole contents of a bottle of chutney, mixing it all together, slicing up the cucumber, with his curiously bent fingers, adding the cream, finally sitting back, with a satisfied little grunt, looking round the table and saying, "Who fresh come from England?"

I ran to and fro with specially composed plates of food for C.M. at the hotel.

When he saw the amount of food on his plate, G. said that "in kitchen they wish I bust", but indeed the kitchen knows only too well that he gives it all to Egout and Poubelle.

At dinner, or at the beginning of it, he was particularly hard to please: everything was wrong. He shouted at everybody in turn, Egout, Poubelle, Marthe, Lise. - Mr. B. told me later that there was an icy blast separating them: I well know that feeling. But as the meal wore on he got less 'angry' with everyone, and during the music was even more than usual ... as he usually is.

He plans another trip, to Cannes this time, and much of the meal was occupied in discussing this.

August 13th

J.G.B. I had my first conversation with Mr. G. about my inner work. I told him enough of the kind of plan I was following to show what I had 'invented' for myself. He said that the physical efforts were quite unnecessary and that I should place all the emphasis on the inner work. He said, "I want you to have real, unperishable 'I' - this must be your aim. Now prepare material. When you have this material I will help you to put in place. Now you are taxi. Every five minutes your 'I' change."

Anyhow he made it clear that he at*tâche*d no value to my bodily suffering as a means of work, although I made it plain that I found a direct and unmistakable benefit from this. But it is, of course quite obvious that such a thing cannot be an aim in itself. My mistake was in thinking that it would provide the 'material' about which he has been speaking to me all the time. Now he has put the task before me in a form which I cannot mistake.

I told him a little about the paper on Unified Field Theory and how it fits in with his 'Law of Falling'. He would have nothing of it - "Mathematik is useless. You cannot learn laws of world creation and world existence by mathematik".

I did not say that my aim had not been just 'cunning wiseacring' but to open a door for scientists to come to his ideas. I was glad I dropped the conversation, for he went on to tell me wonderful things about inner work.

In the afternoon I talked to Frick; then to the Piscine Molitor for a swim with six of the young people.

At dinner G. was very cold towards me at first, but by the end we were as usual together, particularly in the music.

E.B. I met Mr. G. exactly one year ago today.

Tonight we finished 'Material Questions' and went on to 'My Father', which I love. I always look forward to the part about Gilgamesh - "Irrevocably have the Gods resolved to flood the land of Shuripakh".

I forgot to say about last French night that Mr. G. told Mr.

Bennett to be Director at the picnic in the reading room, and I could see, by the reflection in the glass, that they really had it organized.

I sat at the table at lunch. He was very far away from us all, though he suddenly returned in order to tell us a silly story about a 'flying elephant' - how once he saw an elephant sit down on a prickly pear: it leapt up and turned so many somersaults that when it had finished there was nothing left but the tusks.

At dinner he made a tremendous attack on D.P., who was sitting opposite him. I don't know what it all meant, but no doubt she knew. Mr. B. is also in galoshes[1] because he won't give in on the subject of 'material questions'.

Mr. G. and Mme. de S. talked about the movements demonstrations in the Theatre des Champs Elysées, and how the fountains changed their scent every five minutes, and how there were members of the groups 'stopped' on the stairs - particularly those who had friends present!

August 14th

J.G.B. What 24 hours! Yesterday I struggled very hard with the new task he has given me. By not doing the long night and morning tasks, I found myself with very much energy. The result was that I worked hard all day. We also practised the movements from 7.15 to 8.45.

Afterwards I delivered a letter with proofs of 'What are We Living for?' to Frick, and then took E. and Dorothy to drink coffee at the Deux Magots.

Apart from this I was alone all day - I did not go round to the café in the morning, but spent all the time studying and doing my task.

Then the extraordinary thing happened. I read the end of 'The Material Question' and then 'My Father'. Halfway through 'My Father', which I was reading with intimate feeling and aware that G. liked it, suddenly without any warning, I heard an entirely different voice, that I could not recognize at all as my own. 'I' was quite separated from 'him'. I was first surprised at

---

1   In disgrace.

the sound of my voice. Then I thought, "How can he read? 'He' can't possibly give the right intonation". I wondered if people could realize that it was only 'he' reading. 'I' felt wonderfully free and so happy that 'I' was not tied up to 'him'. Then 'he' looked up from the reading at Mr. G. and at the same time I was back again in my body.

The next evening was also extraordinary. At dinner, G. spoke about past, present and future events. At the end of dinner he spoke very harshly to D. Then about her at length in Russian to Mme. de S. Said she had most poisonous emanations and it was not right that he should be exposed to them.

After the music I took D. to the café in the Champs Elysées and we sat and talked until 3 a.m. I advised her to speak freely about everything to Mme. de S. Poor girl, it is a very hard ordeal for her.

I went to bed at 4 a.m. and woke up at 6. I went to sleep again and did not get up till 7. Had a hot bath and dressed. Worked hard on my tasks. I went round to the café at 9.30 and waited for G. He arrived just after 10. I soon had a chance of telling him about last night. He listened very attentively and said, "You work too hard. Such results can be very harmful. Better not work so hard". I said that I could not bear to waste time. I could not stand any longer being only a 'taxi'. He said that it was no use trying to go too fast. I must rest a little. If he had not been there, I might not have been able to get back, and "then go straight in mad house". He spoke some more in the same strain.

Inwardly I felt rebellious and wanted to make double efforts in order to be able to get out more and longer. It could not have lasted more than half a minute judging by the length of the passage I was reading.

I returned to the hotel at 11.45. At 12.15 E. came in and told me of an experience she had last week when he spoke about 'kitchen garden'.

August 15th

J.G.B. Lunch yesterday was a special ordeal. It was clear

from the start that G. intended to make me as drunk as he could. It was the first time he really 'shouted' at me and I was glad to confirm my expectation that I should not feel in the least inwardly disturbed. Anyhow, I had to drink from a large tumbler - half as big as his own. I changed it after the third toast. But we went on right up to Born Idiot, and he and I and Savitsky père, who was Egout, were all very drunk as far as our planetary bodies were concerned.

Lunch began in that way, with one or two violent attacks on me, on the English and so on. But we kept the conversation going and it sometimes touched strange heights. When G. said, "*All* English must become followers of my ideas" I said, "Even Ashiata Shiemash did not expect as much as that. He was satisfied if half tried to work". G. was (I believe) on the point of saying something derogatory about A.S., but stopped himself, and then answered quite seriously, "But Gurdjieff not satisfied. All or nothing". He repeated 'all or nothing' 2 or 3 times.

It was significant to me because it was the first time in my presence that he has made the claim to be the Teacher of our epoch, so clearly. Of course E. has told me that he spoke about 'very few No. 18 ever exist - for example, Ashiata Shiemash was No. 18'. This is equivalent to a direct assertion of equality of 'status'.

His account of the Last Supper, the day before I gave my lecture, implied clearly that he knew of it by direct experience. (At that time I thought he himself had been Judas. Perhaps he was). I remember also his refusal to answer a question about Pentecost, saying, "I do not know; I was not there".

But to return to yesterday's lunch. As time went on, more than once, I knew that he was following my thoughts. Marthe and Lise both wanted me to break up the lunch much earlier, but I knew that he had a purpose and went on as long as he wanted.

Oh, God! How I see the Terror of the Situation. By no means can I work as I should. Even if I make every effort in my power, I only reach states which he says could lead 'straight in mad house'.

Today, driving back with him in his car, I interrogated myself with anguish. I thought, "there are others who suffer more than I do. Some are young and have not wasted their lives as I have. How can I hope to attain what even all these are not attaining? I see the deep rooted pride which has always existed in me, which makes it impossible for me to accept the thought that I should fall behind anyone. I even dare to think that I must try and make the same efforts as G. has made." Then the words of Jesus to the Boanerges came back. "Can ye drink the cup that I drink of?" and they say, "We can, Lord". Also His saying to many of His disciples, perhaps in principle to all, "He that saveth his life ... "; "He that taketh not up his cross ... He that loveth father or mother more than Me is not worthy of Me". How can I be worthy if I do not do all that he has done? And what, in fact, does happen?

I do not carry out even clearly defined tasks which are within my power.

So back to the lunch. He spoke quite a lot about the entry of his ideas into the world. The changed attitude of people towards himself. At first 'like stick in hornet's nest'. But it would not take long to settle down. Then we should all see the effect of the publication of Second Series. But must read Beelzebub first.

Later, when Lonya, Elizabeth and I had taken Savitsky home, we went and had tea in the Bois and really relaxed. I could see that I had to let go some of the tremendous energy that had collected in me. We went on to the movements practice, but most people were still too drunk to work properly. Anyhow the Entwhistles asked us to stop because the concierge was making a fuss about it.

I spoke to Mme. de S. and said I felt rebellious when Mr. G. told me to make fewer efforts. She said, "This is necessary; you cannot force the organism too fast. One or two people in the French group did so and would not listen to him, and had bad results". I said, "But he always drove himself without any pity. Why can I not at least try to make the same efforts?" She said, "No, you are not quite right. Mr. Gurdjieff has always relaxed from time to time. Ever since I have known him, he has had trips and other things just to relax and enjoy himself. If he tells you to relax, you must do it".

In the evening we read 'My First Tutor' and began 'Bogachevsky'.

Dinner was fairly quiet. He told E. she was not to go on the trip, but stay and look after the flat for him. We came away at 2.30 very disinclined for sleep. So we drove out to Versailles. We managed to get into the Trianon gardens and even on a rowing boat on the great Versailles water. We got home at about a quarter to five.

D. came in to breakfast and I talked to her about her personal question and also about education. She is to see Mme. de S. at 12.45.

E.B. The last two days the meals have been very long and very alcoholic. We reached Born Idiots at lunch on Sunday, and in any case most of the conversation was in Russian that day.

Tonight was lovely. We were only 14, and we read from Beelzebub 'Form and Sequence' and 'Impartial Mentation'. Mr. B. reads very well. We finished early, but did not, I am glad to say, start reading anything else. Gurdjieff sat in his armchair by the door, looking round at us, smiling, and said, truth, that not such writing ever was. And as we went in to dinner he said how *'intime'* with so few people, 'very domestic'.

August 16th

J.G.B. The lunch was uneventful. J.D. and his wife were there. They grew stiffer and stiffer and obviously had no use for it all. Gurdjieff himself made an oblique reference to his rôle when he described the Science of Idiotism. He said he was No. 18. When he spoke about "going hup and going down", I said that one could not go higher than No. 17. He said, "No, that is right - from 17 not possible go straight to 18. Necessary once again *descendre jusqu'à ordinaire* and then again consciencely *monter*. Only then can pass to *numero dix-huit*".

After lunch I had a sudden rush of things to do. Savitsky and Lonya to be taken to the Sacré Coeur. Julian Walker to be given lectures. Movements practice to be arranged.

Then D., so utterly devastated by her talk with Mme. de S. How cruel and harsh it seems to us who look on. What she wants with all her heart to be denied her before she has even tasted it, and what she dreads in its weary unendingness, to be sent back to as her only task. I was truly sorry for her, and could not really comfort her. She went off as we were all over the place about the reading. At first it was French night. Then that was canceled. So I fixed to read Beelzebub here in the hotel. Then a message that we were all to go back. We finally settled down at about ten to nine to read 'Electricity' and part of 'Form and Sequence'. Then I was very tired and Miss Crowdy finished it. Then I read 'Impartial Mentation'. Gurdjieff came in almost at once and I could feel how pleased he was to hear it in that small intense circle. When I finished we sat silent for a long time, with a sense of great unity of understanding. Then G. said, "Such chapter! How I write I don't know. I speak *objectivement*. Whether I write or where it come from I don't know. By this chapter the whole force of Beelzebub made three times more."

He was going to say more, when Miss H. entered and he said reproachfully, "See what lecture you miss". She began to explain and he lost all interest and no more happened until the meal, when we came to Hopeless Idiots. He had the Addition and then turned to someone and said that this toast was connected with Impartial Mentation.

After dinner and music I stayed with him and Savitsky and Elizabeth and Marthe. It was one of those strange occasions when he insisted on playing an impossible rôle. He boasted of all the pictures, their amazing age (*plus de 4500 ans*! for a poor copy of a Dutch painting), the enormous prices he paid - how they were all stolen out of museums who are left only with copies, etc. I took up the rôle and towards the end he sat back and let me go on playing it.

We drove all round Paris. We went to the café in the Champs Elysées and talked till nearly 3 a.m., then drove round the Bois still talking and arrived back at the hotel at 4 a.m. E. said that she felt she had no personal rôle in all this: that she might get something out of it, but that was up to her. She was not part of the plan. That we are all 'cannon-fodder' and that it is up to us whether we feed a pop-gun or a real cannon.

E.B. At the end of the evening, Lise being away, I waited till everyone had gone except Mr. B., Savitsky and Marthe, who were in Gurdjieff's small sitting room with him, in case I was able to do something for him. I stood in the passage, reading the part about the Pyramids in the New Model, which someone had left lying about. Then Mr. B. came out and said why didn't I come too and have some coffee, which of course I did. It was interesting to see Mr. G. start the proceedings and then withdraw and leave it to Mr. B.

August 17th

J.G.B. I struggled yesterday as I suppose I never struggled with myself before. I remember nothing of what was said or done at lunch, except that I had gone to fetch Mme. de S., and arrived late. Marianne was reading 'Good and Evil' and I sat down on my knees to listen. The reading went on for 1 1/2 hours and I was in acute pain for the last half hour. G. came in during the reading and listened with great attention. I had the feeling that he prolonged the reading because he knew that I was in pain. Anyhow, he let Marianne read to the end of the chapter, which he seldom does.

After the Movements, we had only 'Fragments' to read. I hated the thought of reading it, but I took Chapter V and forced myself to read. G. soon came in and showed that he was interested in hearing it. So I thought, 'at least there is benefit to somebody', and began to make myself read well. We did not read long, and went in to dinner with an unusually large party for these days - say 30 people. G. was in wonderful form all the evening. I was at first so negative and seething inside that I only wanted one thing in the world - to go off and be alone.

But again I made myself be cheerful and very soon the rôle began to play itself, although inwardly I kept remembering. When it came to Round Idiots (i.e. Page, 'Sausage' and myself), he turned to me and said, "Your health, Director, also". I said, "I need it". He then went on to speak about angels and devils. I asked him to introduce me to just one devil. He said, "This very expensive thing is. Costet at least 4 *zéros*". I said that I would pay, anyhow "3 *zéros* with hunchback". He said, "Not enough; must be 4 *zéros*". I understood that he meant that I must first by my own efforts make something firm and unchangeable in myself and then he could help that something to become conscious and free to act.

Later he spoke to Lonya about having a task of sleeping only six and a half hours each night. Lonya asked if he could come to it gradually, but G. said, "No". He also asked, "How long must I do it?" Then G.'s eyes flashed with that terrible fire of his and he said almost in a shout, "Forever!"

He went on to say that you can never give things up gradually. "It is like smoking. No one can stop this little by little, necessary decide and then do. For two, three days it is easy, but fourth day very difficult. Afterwards must struggle. Then it can be done."

He turned to me, and said, "Good formulation, not?" and with those words, I felt the door shut and I was shut in Purgatory until I have purified myself.

Afterwards I drove Mme. de S. and Marthe home. I did not say anything to her. There is no more to say. I went back to the Avenue Carnot and saw Keith and Rina sitting together and several of the others just behind. After a short talk with them the café closed (about 2.30 a.m.) and they walked towards the hotel. I took the car and drove to Versailles and back. Arrived home at 3.30 and went to bed. I look back at the absurdity of my life and say to myself, 'You thought you were an intelligent man!' Indeed only Mullah Nassr Eddin could do justice to my feeling about myself.

At lunch Lemaître was there, and G. said in a pleased tone, "Ah! Real Director!" I sat as *Champ d'épandage*[1] next to Keith. Mme. de S. was there.

At the end of lunch came the strange experience - there had been much talk of money matters, G.'s immediate needs and so

1   Sewage Farm.

on. Then (à propos of what I cannot remember) he announced that he could write a cheque with 7 *zéros* - "Even your King cannot do that!" His bank would at once honour such a cheque. At first I thought he was joking, when suddenly I realized that he was speaking specially to me and no one else was realizing. I said to him that it must be a special bank. He said, yes, only allow people who can write cheque with at least 6 *zéros*. This made his meaning perfectly clear, but to confirm it to myself I said, "Such a bank can have only very few clients". He said, yes, but now they make big *réclame*. Two or three more sentences were added, including his saying "for a long time now I can write cheque with 7 *zéros*".

I was naturally overwhelmed at being told such a thing, and what is more by his taking the trouble to make the precise meaning of the symbolism so clear.

As we were going out of the room a minute later, he looked (or pretended to look) for his cigarettes and matches which were just beside him. I leaned over and gave them to him and he said, "You are *very* intelligent". Keith who was beside me naturally thought he was referring to my noticing that he wanted his cigarettes. Keith told me afterwards that he had felt something very strange in the conversation, but could make absolutely nothing of it.

That is the fifth or sixth time that he has told me and evidently he means that I should act on it. That is one reason why I put the quotation from Schweitzer at the beginning of the book[1].

August 18th

J.G.B. This was the day of the abortive trip to Vichy and the caves of Lascaux. I was very tired and did not know how I would stand it. But I slept a little in the morning and felt better. I had a slight accident, probably due to fatigue. The 'trip' ended at Corbeille, when G.'s clutch ceased to work. We returned to Paris at 6.

At dinner several new people came. I read 'I AM'. Then a

1   J. G. Bennett, *What Are We Living For?*, Hodder & Stoughton, 1949.

very gay dinner with much good food, including an omelette with red caviar.

I took Marthe and Luba home and went back to bed at 3.30.

August 19th

J.G.B. Lunch today was notable for G.'s wonderful addition to Zigzag Idiots. He spoke about Unchangeable 'I' and Immortality. A greater commandment than the ten given to Moses. Mme. de S. and I had to translate and explain. "You see that I dare to say such things!"

This evening, after 1 1/2 hours' good work on the movements with Emil, sitting at the café on the Place des Ternes with Bernard and Kyril Koupenik, I was suddenly penetrated through and through with the realization that I had to sacrifice more than my own desires ... I have to face the fact that I cannot expect to do without my cake and expect it to remain uneaten.

August 20th

J.G.B. I realize more bitterly than ever before in my life that I have no being. I see through and through that I am still on the level of ordinary being. For some reason, I have glimpses of a different experience, but 'I' remain just where I was. I have set before myself tasks really difficult and very painful, both morally and physically. I have had wonderful help. And yet I remain where I was. But for Mr. G., I think I should fall into a bleak and hopeless pessimism. But he shows that the goal can be reached.

E.B. All these days, and I have written nothing! But for 2 days I couldn't write - it was all I could do to appear at meals twice a day. I felt that I had ruined everything.

The other day at lunch, Mr. G. began to talk about his bank, at which no one could have an account who could not write a cheque with 6 *zéros*. He had for long been able to write a cheque for 7 *zéros*, and what he could do before he could do now. All this was addressed to Mr. B., who was sitting exactly in front of me, and I didn't really understand it, but only thought here was a strange *zéro* talk, with something that I could not understand.

He gave Lonya a task 'forever!' of not sleeping for more than 6 ½ hours in 24. When L. asked if he could do this gradually, he said no, necessary begin at once. Like giving up smoking: the first two days are easy, the third and fourth days are difficult, but it is necessary to cut it off at once, not gradually.

I have now an acute dislike of the food at the flat - this has become steadily worse in the last 2 or 3 months - since I had jaundice, I think. It is all I can do to eat it, and sometimes it all comes back and I have to swallow it over again, like a cow.

Mr. G. was going to Vichy on a trip, and he was going to leave me and Rina in charge of the flat, to sleep there, etc. He gave us many instructions about it and said, "Not forget - I trust you" (he pronounces it 'trest').

When the trip was called off, owing to a slipping clutch, he made a wonderful dish for dinner that night; an omelette with salmon caviare, and made little jokes about "how much better air in Vichy - you not remember how was in Paris this morning?" and said how Rina and I were 'disillusioned' by his return.

That night when nearly everyone had gone, I was kneeling on the floor beside his chair, asking if he wanted anything before I left, when M. came, and took his hand and kissed it, and said goodnight. When she had gone, he smiled at me, and said, speaking very quietly, "She wished speak with me, but what can I say to her? I have nothing say". I said, "That must happen often". "Very often, yes. Such idiot, what can I do?"

He spoke very seriously last night to Bernard about being a 'doctor in quotation marks'.

He has looked wonderful lately. He has been wearing a strange sort of garment like a pyjama jacket, of a bright pale turquoise blue: this, with his dark red fez and his brown face, is very becoming.

Keith Thorburn has been Egout twice a day for a week - he had half a sheep's head at three meals running, poor him!

Yesterday as I was driving her in the car, Mme. de S, said he is "very sympathetic for Egout".

Tonight when we reached Hopeless Idiots G. was very solemn and after the Addition, spoke about 'this small aim' not to perish like a dog, and how everyone must have this. Everyone must have the wish 'not be taxi', but to have real owner, not a succession of passengers. He gave us all the task of learning to distinguish between feeling and sensing - when he sees that we do this task, and do it often, then he will be able to give us another subjective task.

I drove Mme. de S. home today and she spoke about Mr. B. How he tries experiments, and this is good. How this is only till he is free; then he can do what he likes. How if I behave properly in this it will be good for me: how I understand differently since I came. What an extraordinary relationship this is, how life near Mr. G. is not easy for *anyone*, how with all one's suffering one would not wish any other way, but this is 'more expensive'.

I am writing this early: I woke full of uneasiness after a very unquiet night, very much afraid for Mr. B.

August 21st

J.G.B. I have just returned after driving out nearly to Mantes. I left the flat at 2 p.m. in a state of despair because I had drunk so much that I had no chance of collecting my attention. Now I have made it worse by tiring myself to exhaustion as well. This morning I continued to work at the exercise up to six times. Then I went to see Gurdjieff at the café and afterwards to the apartment. I told him the whole of the events of the night.

He said that this was one half of what he wanted from me. From now it would be easy to return to that state, but impossible until my energy was replenished. I must sleep.

He explained that the organism does not itself want nor can it get anything from the work. I must be just to it.

The conversation gave me encouragement. For the first time, he said explicitly that I had made a right step forward.

Later. The sequence of events since yesterday is so

important to me that I must try to write them down. First of all when I spoke with G. he was emphatic about the need for sleep. "For your typicality six hours sleep is necessary. Go back now and sleep till half past one and then come lunch".

He also told me that after I had once reached this, the state I wanted would come easily in future. This 'come easily' he emphasized in a way that meant nothing more to me then. He spoke about the 'organism'. It did not want to develop, it had no aim, it could not reach anything for itself, so it was necessary to be just to it, not make it suffer without reason.

I half saw that he referred not only to my body but to the whole of my present existence, but this may be fancy. After all my mind has an aim, so perhaps he referred to the bodily existence only. Anyhow, I went off feeling very disturbed and excited. I looked forward to doing the task really well at night (having quite failed to make real to myself what he had said about sleep). It did not enter my head that something could have been achieved during the rest period. Anyhow, I went to lunch and nothing much happened to me personally. There were many people there. At every meal now G. says wonderful things, but I forget them. At some meal recently he drank my health as Doubting Idiot, which astonished me. By the way, on Friday, during the music after lunch, the garage men arrived from Corbeille with his car. He called them in, paid them from his own pocket, gave them Armagnac to drink and told me to put away his car. Then yesterday when I arrived at the café he said he was waiting for me to telephone to see why his car had not come. When I told him it had been delivered the previous day, he assured me he had completely forgotten all about it. This so struck him that he repeated it to Mme. de S. at lunch.

Anyhow, after lunch I went to the Salle Pleyel to book a studio for movements practice and then drove round the Bois, having in mind the 'relaxation' G. had recommended. We did the movements fairly exhaustingly and then I returned to the hotel and slept until dinner time.

At dinner Gurdjieff spoke to me unmistakably about remorse, and the need to turn remorse into work. He spoke also about the greatness of our aim and how he was only waiting to help anyone who would prepare the ground so that he could plant the seed in him.

(By the way, in his private talk with me in the morning, he spoke about the state I had reached as yeast. This would now ferment the whole dough and enable bread to be made from it.)

After the music I lingered in the room, even though G. several times told me to go and sleep. I was so obtuse that even then I could not understand. Finally I left the flat at about 2 a.m. Several people - Keith especially and Bernard - were waiting below to ask me questions. I answered as briefly as I could. They went up to the café and I took the car and drove off towards Versailles and Mantes. At about 2.45 I stopped the car in absolute stillness, with the Milky Way shining above my head. I struggled with the exercise, but failed completely. I then lay in the back of the car and slept for half an hour. Then I drove back to Paris, arriving at 4.30 a.m. I went to bed and slept. I woke up at about 7.30 and to my complete amazement found myself in the state I had struggled for, without any effort. This was repeated twice more. At last I understood what G. had been saying about sleep and the 'easy arrive next time'. I stayed in bed till nearly 9 o'clock, when people began to disturb me.

E.B. We read 'From the Author' before lunch. I have never understood it so well, never been so moved by it or so filled with horror at my situation. Mr. B. read very well. I am glad to say that Mr. G. has told him to sleep.

I looked back at what I had written yesterday about Hopeless Idiots and realized that I hardly touched the most important part, when Mr. G. talked about 'I AM', and how when one had this one could work for 'unchangeable I' and pay for one's existence.

August 22nd

J.G.B. I have been resting a great deal and taking things easily. Yesterday after lunch I slept for three hours. At 9 p.m. I had a cold bath and then decided to make a big effort with my task. I knelt for an hour - 20 minutes with arms out sideways - and the first half hour I made the utmost effort to reach and keep the necessary state. I did not succeed, but I did the exercise better than before. A few days ago I should have called it very successful, and I felt inwardly refreshed and in a good state. Only now I have the hunger for the real state, and fear I shall not get it back!

Yesterday I drank 'honourably' and G. continued very long - right up to Patented Idiot. I went to the café afterwards in the Champs Elysées with Keith, Charles N. and several others. Then drove Sophia and Elizabeth back to the hotel. I slept extremely heavily and woke up with a headache and could not do my exercise at all. I remained heavy and drowsy until after 10 o'clock. I made one or two efforts to free myself from the effects of the alcohol I had drunk the night before, but it was not until just before lunch that I began to feel normal.

I did not read well. It was the end of 'From the Author' and the beginning of 'Yelov'. Lunch was a quiet meal. G. also was very tired and sleepy. I know that several people had gone round to the café to see him this morning. I felt a recurrent inner indignation at the way people impose on him. I say to myself that I try not to do so, but I am no better than the rest.

After lunch I drove Mme. de S. home and told her briefly about what had happened to me. I said that my chief fear was that I would not be able to repeat this and make it my own. This is above all what I long for now. It is a clear and definite aim. I want to be able to reach that state by some sequence of efforts or actions which I shall know how to make. That is why I am frightened of this 'rest period'. Am I going to lose touch with what I found? Mme. de S. assured me that this would not be so, and that I must really relax for the next few days. If not she said I might have bad consequences. By the way, I drank scarcely anything at lunch. G. noticed, but said nothing.

After leaving Mme. de S. I returned to the flat and heard the music being played back. It was very melancholy. Just as it finished, Lise returned, and G. was so obviously delighted to see her again that it made us all happy. He told her that the melancholy music had been composed on her account. At lunch I called E.'s toast of Square Idiot and she looked at me and bowed slightly, unsmiling. Gurdjieff at once said, "Yelizabet, why you not manifest? When Director gives toast, necessary manifest pleasure. Perhaps you are angry with Director?" She assured him that she was not, and he repeated that she must 'manifest pleasure'. Then as she was saying goodbye before leaving for England, he pointed to me and said, "You speak with him before you go".

It is a mystery to me, his knowledge of what we all do with our lives in his absence. Again and again people confirm this quite unmistakably.

I forgot to say that last night when I left the flat, Keith said to me, "Did G. speak at the end of the meal to Mme. de S. in Russian or in French?" "In Russian". He said, "I thought so. But I understood the whole thing perfectly, although I don't know a word of Russian."

E.B. I had lunch at the flat and afterwards went to England. At lunch, when we came to Square Idiots, Mr. Gurdjieff was looking at me all through the preliminaries "We come now to the series ... " I knew he had something up his sleeve. I was in my corner by the piano, and Bouche d'Egout obscured my view of the Director, who said, "To your health also, Elizabeth ... " I looked away from Mr. G. to the Director; leaned forward just enough to see him and gave a small nod. The Director had already looked away from me. Mr. G. was still looking at me when I turned back to him again, and then he said, kind and amiable and only half serious, that when one's health is drunk, necessary something manifest, and how this is serious thing, etc. He added, "perhaps something happen between you and Director, I not know, but necessary something manifest".

Lise returned after lunch - he was very pleased to see her.

August 23rd

J.G.B. 8.45 a.m. IN THE PLANE FOR NICE Bernard came to see me off at the airport, very excited because G. had said that he could become a real doctor by coming and working near to him - G. - for 2 or 3 years.

I must make it clear to myself what I really want. Certainly I want greater mastery over my body. I have nearly complete mastery over it already. I know that this will come of itself now, if l continue to work. I am not afraid of physical pain, I can resist physical desires, overcome physical aversions, do without sleep or food and so on.

Certainly also I want to *know* more, but as with the body I already have so much knowledge that I can be sure that this will steadily increase. I am still very far from understanding the complexity of the human psyche, but this is the most difficult of all, because it is so near to the chaotic that scarcely any laws or general principles can be found. Only immense practical experience can help. The knowledge I want cannot come suddenly by some intensive effort.

So, the feelings. Do I want less feeling? Or more feeling? Or different feeling? I believe I want more feelings, but not to be slave to them. To be able to suffer consciously and intentionally. Gradually my feelings will be purified as something else comes into my nature.

Then what is this 'something else'? I find myself at once at a loss.

None of this can make sense of my life - it does not correspond to the 'sense and meaning of my existence'. In other words, let me put aside 'philosophizing' about aim. Let me do the utmost I can to master that state and gain control over my hanbledzoin.

August 24th

J.G.B. Well, I gave my lecture in Italian and it was as successful as one could possibly expect. Many people thanked me, including Dr. Montessori herself. I spoke to her after her own lecture. Her humility is a wonderful and beautiful property. She said to me, "You value me much too highly. I want to learn from you." I arranged to go to Holland in October to see her.

The lecture was summarized on the Italian wireless and the

Times correspondent (who asked me how to spell 'Gurdjieff!') told me he was sending a fairly full report to London, but naturally nothing will be published there!

August 25th

    E.B. I arrived in time to go to the flat for dinner. C. and B.C.M. met me. I was so *glad* to be there again. Mr. G. noticed that I was back and so did Mme. de S. - in fact the only person who appeared not to notice was Mr. B.

    I have made a strict plan for myself in the week ahead of me. If I do not work this week, with such constant reminders, I may as well give up and take to needlework, drugs or lovers - or anything else: it seems that there is no direction in which I could not have more success than I have in this.

    When Mr. G. was talking tonight about Katherine Mansfield, Mme. de S. told him that they have put up a plaque in her memory on the Prieuré wall,[1] "but not yet to M. Gurdjieff". Mr. B. told the story about the bath being said to be built by the *Saints Russes*, and Mr. G. was much amused.

August 26th

    J.G.B. I arrived at le Bourget, found a returning taxi and came straight back, thus missing Bernard, who had come to meet me at the Invalides. Took Jimmy, C.M. and R.H. out to coffee and told them about San Remo. At 9.30, set off with Bernard, C.M. and E.M., but saw Mr. G. in his café, so I let them go on alone and had a long talk with him. He was very pleased with the mention of his work on the Italian radio! We talked till 10.15 and returned together to the apartment. I came to the hotel to wash and went back in time to read the 'Warning'. We did not get very far before dinner. The main feature of dinner was (for me) the sense of the changed inner relationship between Mr. G., Mme. de S. and myself. He spoke a good deal in Russian, evidently bringing us closer together.

    There was one unexpected moment. At Hopeless Idiots, Cathleen's was the only toast, and when I drank her health,

---

1   Katherine Mansfield died at the Prieuré.

Mr. G. pricked his ears and said, "Who? Where?" Mme. de S. pointed to Cathleen and he said, "Oh. I thought you said Katherine Mansfield. She my friend. But she die. So I astonished what you repeat that name. She my good friend."

The dinner finally led me to much talk about *zéros*. He turned to me and said, "I give you *tâche*, which will serve as reminding factor. I must have 3 *zéros* with hunchback. That will remind you, day, night. Also for me will be useful." He then used some Russian word, which I understood to mean 'laying a burden'. He said, 'no', and made a gesture of tying up a parcel. He told Mme. de S. to find a translation and we talked for some time about it when the lights went out, and when the fuse was repaired the conversation had changed. After dinner there was short, but really wonderful, music.

When I returned I worked at my exercise for an hour, finishing at 3.30. There came to my mind a saying of Miss C. "Bennett is too weak with G. You will see that he will suck him dry." I thought of my talk with Mme. de S., and I recognized that this scheme is really the one I talked over with her. She must have told him about it. So that the suggestion really came from me and he has accepted it in the form of a 'task'. In that way everyone benefits. But all the same, I must not in the least forget that with Gurdjieff weakness is punished as a deadly sin. But above all I rejoice in my own 'I'. Never until this morning could I be quite sure of this. But ever since I woke this morning I have experienced it, and because of it I can know how I shall behave in the future.

At lunch G. spoke about the two streams of life and how active one must be to hold one's place in the living water.

E.B. Spent the morning with Mr. Savitsky and Mme. Farman in the Rue de l'Assomption, choosing a tricot. I chose one of Jacques Fath's designs and felt very pleased with myself. Much chat about the '*mode actuelle*' and so on. Strange to have a conversation like that again.

There was a strange little incident at dinner when the Director drank to "your health also, Cathleen Murphy". Mr. G.

thought he said "Katherine Mansfield" and said, "she my good friend", but she was dead, so how could this be?

There was much talk about the *château*, and much talk between Mr. G., Mme. de S. and the Director in Russian, and much *zéro* talk - he gave Mr. B. the task of collecting "3 *zéros* with hunchback" while G. is in America. This will be useful for self-remembering; "not much will sleep with such *tâche*", And also useful for him, Mr. G.

There was beautiful music afterwards, short and with a very abrupt end - lovely.

August 27th

J.G.B. After lunch today I slept for 3 ½ hours, missing the movements practice with Alfred, for which I was very sorry. But I was refreshed and able to do my duty at the meal and afterwards very much better. The dinner was exceptional. Gurdjieff sat till 2 at the table and we did not leave the apartment till 3. He was not particularly tired and invited several people to his little room.

At dinner I felt all the time the force of his presence. After he had called several people to his room and given them chocolates and spoken to them, I stayed after they had left and said goodbye to him. "You continue to do the task I give you and I promise you will not have passenger, but Real 'I' on your motor car". I said that I knew this stupid sort of compassion in myself, which makes me want to help people without knowing how. He said, yes, but will not do in future.

Afterwards I went with Col. Flower and young Thomas Adie to the café in the Champs Elysées, I had been with Flower at the Musée de l'Homme in the morning and spoken to him about the change in humanity at the Middle Aurignacian period.

I reflected a great deal upon my present position. Have I allowed my imagination to run away with me? It is characteristic of me to treat the first hurdle as if it were the winning post.

Alas that I cannot hope to record the last 20 hours. I have suffered so much and heard and learnt so much. But I cannot remember it all. As part of my task, I had a conversation with Mr. G. in which I spoke of everything except myself and the burning questions to which I need an answer. I spent about an hour with him before lunch. At lunch he spoke about Hopeless Idiots and said that if one set oneself the aim of dying honourably, he could show us how to be unmortal, and, looking directly at me, he said, "Unmortal; that is big thing. And that is not all, for you can become one of those Beings who are significant even for our God".

He spoke at length about the animalcules in a drop of water and compared man on earth to such small things. Ordinary people did not and could not exist for God or even for the angels. He said to one person, "you are so small that even the smallest devil cannot see you". The majestic picture he drew of the difference between ordinary beings and Great Beings struck awe into my heart. I was filled with remorse for the wretched efforts I make.

We are apparently to go on a trip tomorrow.

E.B. Today Mr. B. leant down from Olympus, scolded me for several faults which we have in common, and withdrew again. If he would scold me without being so patronizing about it, I wouldn't get so angry, but when he carps at my behaviour to other people, as though he himself has the key to the whole works, I feel nothing but irritation, knowing so well how he falls down on his treatment of other people. But there ...

At every meal the last two days Mr. G. has spoken about Hopeless Idiots. How this is a good formulation which everyone can understand; how this is the least aim we can set ourselves and, at lunch on Friday, the analogy of the two streams of the river of life. I can't reproduce the wonderful things he has said.

Colonel Flower arrived on Friday and was Egout for his first two meals. He seems to fit in and belong here after only 2 days.

At lunch today, Mr. G. talked about the life in a drop of water, and how God cannot know each individual, and how futile are the sort of prayers we pray - "please, God, make husband give me ... " and a delicious pantomime of putting on a fur coat. How the beings in a drop of water are as we are - they work, eat, sleep - even have God, even perhaps pray to their God.

At the end of the meal as he was leaving the room, Gurdjieff asked me if I understood something he had been saying to Mr. B., (in fact I had understood but thought I didn't agree!) and he said I must study his ideas for two more years: then I would understand.

Tonight he talked about eating and food, and how eating with other people is a fundamental part of life. How this is a - not ceremony, not ritual - I forget the word - which Christ performed, and which he performs here, and afterwards someone else will sit in his place and this will go on. But, turning to Mr. B., Judas was the really important rôle in this. "Because of Judas, your Christ has been God for 2,000 years". Sometimes it was better to pray to Judas than to pray to God. When he is drunk he prays to Judas. "But then I all times drunk", so he always prays to Judas.

August 28th

J.G.B. NEVERS First day of trip. This morning several of us got together to reconstruct what G. has said about the rôle of Judas. Not only was Judas the direct and efficient cause of Jesus being, for 2,000 years, God to half mankind, but his was the supreme rôle. "I do not often pray to God. I do not wish disturb His Endlessness. But when I am drunk, I pray to Judas." A pause. "And I am nearly always drunk". He spoke very extravagantly about the rôle of Judas, as the only one really conscious self-sacrificing rôle. The truly Great One of the Christian event. Of Jesus as "only a little Jew", and so on. Separating that which was said merely to shock newcomers, there remains the consistent teaching of Judas as playing an all-important part without which Christianity as we know it would not have existed. Then why publish Beelzebub now? Why not wait for a "sign"?

But the trip has started. In G.'s car were, at first, Mrs.

Nicholls and John; E.M. and Marianne. In my car, Lise, Tim Dahlberg and Mrs. von Harten. After about 80 km, Elizabeth and Lise changed places. We had one breakdown after another - tyres, lights, etc. - but we all arrived together at Nevers. There was not much gaiety at dinner, but the tiredness of everyone had something to do with it.

E.B. NEVERS Today we started on the trip to Vichy. I was in Mr. G.'s car for the first hour, but then he called for Lise, thinking she was in the back of the car. When he was told she was with Mr. B., he was from then on not able to rest and when we stopped for coffee, I asked him if I should change with her, and he said yes. So I went back to Mr. B.'s car, where were Mrs. Dahlberg and Mrs. von Harten. (This was a curious trip: Iovanna and I were the only members of the party who had been on a trip before. There was a large contingent of older women who were embarked on their first trip with Mr. G.) The car had *many* breakdowns - tyres, and then lights and what-not, and driving was very tricky. Mr. B. never knew when the lights were going to fail. But we caught up with Mr. G.'s car before Nevers - he does not see well for driving fast at night - and arrived together.

We dined alone in the restaurant at about 10.30. We were all more or less tired and G. said very little, but enjoyed the food.

August 29th

J.G.B. VICHY - We left Nevers at 9. Lise had driven most of the way and once again demonstrated her amazing power of observation and execution. She drove for two hours with almost complete assurance, after only ten lessons in the Bois de Boulogne.

Later. After lunch I went out shopping with E.M. and Mrs. Dahlberg. When we returned at about 5 p.m. I struggled with my task.

We all went with Gurdjieff to his café. Then to dinner. Once again he spoke about Zigzag Idiots.

Continued at mid-day. He spoke about our Inner God, and some vague understanding moved in me but I spoiled it by the wrong association. I asked him how one can get an 'Inner Devil'. He replied that for this I would have to pay 'three *zéros*'. I at once pulled out my pocket book and offered to write a cheque, saying, "I am surprised that you make it so cheap. I expected you to ask for five *zéros*"! He said, "five *zéros* later on". But he would say no more. Yet I knew he was giving me a hint of something tremendously important. He spoke about only letting himself eat when he '*mérite*'. It so happened that a minute or two before this conversation I had decided not to eat the very delicious chicken they had served because I felt I was allowing myself to enjoy the food too much 'like pig'. I suppose he noticed this, but he gave no sign. He went on to say that there was a second person inside him whom he always asked if he had merited anything, and only if this second person said that he had merited then he could enjoy.

He spoke also about the zigzag idiot with a thousand 'I's, all with their own desires and impulses. But the zigzag idiot can work by using all these as a reminding factor. "If he does this, then I admire him with all my presence! But ordinary zigzag idiot with five Fridays in the week is only shit of shit." He clarified, in answer to a question from Iovanna, that there is nothing special about Friday. "Sunday is the same".

In another conversation (or rather it was part of the one about the Inner God), he spoke of the Ten Commandments. They cannot help a man to work. But if he listens to his Inner God, then he has something a thousand times greater than the Ten Commandments. He said to the others, pointing to me, "Only he understand this conversation. You all not yet understand. He will explain you." It concerned the denial of one's own natural impulses. The value of this as a reminding factor.

He went off to bed very early, just after eleven. About nine people came with me to his café and asked me to explain about the above conversation. As I was speaking, I was reflecting that I can speak so well to a *number* of people and I nearly always go wrong with individuals. I wonder why this is so.

At about midnight most of the people returned to the hotel, and the rest of us sat and talked till nearly 2.30. Then I went to my, room and began an hour's task. It went so wonderfully well that I knew I had an altogether new power over my organism. When it came to the fifteen minute arms-out-sideways I felt as if my arms were supported by an invisible power. I was able to go right through without using exercises to keep my attention. I have *always* had to use them before.

E.B. I came down early, had breakfast and then kept an eye on the loading of the cars. We left at 9 and this time, once we were clear of the town, Lise drove the Vauxhall for two hours, as far as the outskirts of Vichy. She is an astonishing girl. The train party arrived after lunch, so we are now 15.

Peggy Flinch arrived at midnight.

At lunch G. complained about the tastelessness of the trout, but commended the frying of the potatoes and sent for the boy who had cooked them - "not chef" - to congratulate him.

In the evening at the café, he sent the "young" away to find out what theatres, cabarets etc. were to be seen in Vichy. At dinner he said he was going to bed now, as he was very tired and Mrs. Mills could also go to bed, but the "young" could go to a cabaret. He turned to John M. and said, "You perhaps also wish go?" John said, no, and Mr. G. asked, "Why? Because mother not go?" Yes, said John, that is why. Mr. G. said this was good; good to want to stay with mother. But also this could be bad: it was necessary to experience everything. How could you experience good if you had not also experienced evil? Good to go to a cabaret and see how people behave, and think very often to oneself, I AM. He said something that I couldn't grasp about the Commandments of Moses, and how if we listened to our Inner God we would have something even more powerful.

He said that he only allows himself to eat something "when I mérite".

When he had gone to bed, about a dozen of us went to a café and Mr. B. talked about the Science of Idiotism.

August 30th

J.G.B. I did not sleep, so I got up at 7.30 and meditated very intensely.

I met Gurdjieff at the café. We went together to the Baths and had '*massage sous l'eau*'. Walking back with him, I was aware that there was not one but two people inside me. I left him at the café and went back to the hotel to do various jobs. As I was walking back, thinking about the task I had set myself, suddenly the thought flashed into my mind, "But of course, this Unchangeable 'I' about which we speak must be and can only be a spark of God's own essence. All I need to do is to provide a vehicle for it." This obvious fact which I have heard so many times came to me like a revelation. I saw the whole situation of the Three Bodies of Man and the 'I' which is God himself seated in the highest body.

E.B. Before lunch today, Mr. Gurdjieff distributed 'solid scent' to us all. B.C.M. told me of a conversation he had in the café this morning, before the *massage sous l'eau*. (The men went off together and the women made a separate party). Bernard asked Mr. G. whether one should study Freud and Jung, and he said, no, no; this only masturbation. One should learn massage in German Switzerland, and one would do well to study Braid and Mesmer on hypnotism ...

At dinner there was a most exciting conversation, and tantalizing, because I could not understand it, and nor could anyone else when I asked afterwards: all had some *reason* for not having heard, or simply admitted that they had not understood. (I said both). B.C.M., next to Mr. B., heard most, but that wasn't much. This is how it seemed to me to be.

À propos something or other, Mr. B. said that when he was very young, in Constantinople, he had on one occasion, when blind drunk, ruined 50 water melons and broken the top of a marble-topped table, remembering nothing afterwards. Mr. G. at once snapped this up to hang on it an obviously already-thought-out piece of teaching: he began to talk about immortality. How from one's work one can build up something 'unmortal' and how it is necessary to experience everything, even under the influence of drink. If one can remember what happens then, so much the better. He went on to say that Mr. B. already has his Kesdjan body, but this is not really immortal. He must not be satisfied with this. Real immortality comes only with the third body. Then something I could not understand about the distinction between the life of the *'soleil absolu'* and the life of paradise, which can only be for a time. *Not be satisfied.* Imagine how dreadful to have paradise year in and year out for ever (not his words, of course, but this is how I understood). Then, this is very simple. Only necessary work. How work? Well, only by saying I AM not less than once every hour. From this everything can come.

Johnny Nicholls *snatched* rather when the water-melon came round, and Mr. G. said how bad this was; that when he was a child they had had water melon only once a year - he could remember his father serving it once a year. It is better, he said, to start poor. This is not 'cheap thing'.

To bed quite early.

August 31st

J.G.B. At dinner, suddenly, out of the blue, as happens when Mr. G. intends to say something carefully premeditated, he began to speak to me about immortality. "There are two kinds unmortal. You now already have Kesdjan body, this is unmortal, but not real unmortal. Real unmortal only comes with higher body. You have body for soul, but must have body for 'I' ".

He then spoke of the distinction between Paradise and *Soleil Absolu*. You can go to Paradise with the Kesdjan body. But Paradise is only good for two or three days. "Imagine what would be if next year, year after, hundred years. Imagine how you would be 'irked' (not the word, but equivalent), by such thing. Must want go *Soleil Absolu.*"

I understood perfectly everything that he meant by this. It corresponds exactly with all that I had been thinking about during the day.

I remembered the saying, "When he has crystallized, he can have whatever he wants". I know that I *can* have whatever I want, but I will not take it.

Most unmistakably my aim has changed, even before he spoke. Until now, I have desired and striven for mastery over my physical organism, including my thoughts and feelings. I have wanted to reach the assurance that 'I' was free from my planetary body. All day today I have lived with that assurance. And at the same time I have become more and more obsessed with the need to make myself a vehicle for the Will of God. Or able to receive and be part of His Essence.

Now I must sleep. I am very tired. I have written a long letter to Mme. Ouspensky.

E.B. We left at 9 and had a marvellous drive through Clermont Ferrand and by the Puy de Dome to Montdore. I thought it very beautiful. Mr. B.'s car led. Five people had hired a car at Vichy in order to come too. We stopped at Montdore for lunch, an excellent lunch, which Mr. B. had ordered in advance. Mr. G. complained that his tape-worm was not interested in the proceedings, but the food was very good and he was able to eat quite a good lunch in the end. He told about how the Chinese bury eggs for 25 years before eating them, and the story about the Roquefort cheese running away, and how, after the first mouthful, "if wish repeat", it was necessary to be quick, or the cheese would have run away. Then he said quite seriously that this was a good thing; invertebrates make the right food for man.

We went on to Montignac, stopping somewhere or other to sleep in a wood of beautiful tall trees, and arrived at about 9. G. was very tired. He, Lise, the three Nicholls and Bernard slept at the Soleil d'Or, where we all had a great welcome from the Bourgs. Mr. B. slept in one of those old houses on piles over the river, and the rest of us were in two other houses in the village: Tim, the two Mills, the chauffeur of the hired car and I were in one house and the rest in another.

We had dinner at the Soleil d'Or at about 9.30. Gurdjieff

had played a pleased rôle at lunch; now he played a displeased one, pretending that everything was wrong. He ate very little, though he enjoyed an excellent ice cream. The same little old woman, like a merry mouse, waited on us, and he was very kind to her and praised the Bourgs, who had taken great trouble. He talked little, being so tired. A little about religion - the Orthodox had retained at least something; Roman Catholicism had degenerated entirely, etc.; the Anglicans were stupid because their rituals had nothing for the children.

And a horrid story about the worms in our insides - "not alone *solitaire*",[1] but also four others, like snakes, and the revolting methods necessary to get rid of them, reminding me of the over-amorous wife in the Arabian Nights, who had to be held over a steam kettle!

When G. had gone to bed at about midnight, Mr. B. and I sat in the garden for a while, talking over the events of the day. Then he walked back to the hotel with me, and on the way we swam in the river. But I have never fancied that stretch of the river since the night I found a new-born dead baby in it. I went to bed about 1.45. Very hot, but the bed very comfortable!

September 1st

J.G.B. 6 p.m. ON THE WAY BACK TO PARIS We visited the caves (of Lascaux) this morning. Gurdjieff accepted their authenticity and antiquity, except that he put their age at 8,000 years instead of the 18-20,000 of the prehistorians. I shall try later on to write down all that he said.

E.B. Gurdjieff would not eat any breakfast. While we had ours, in the garden of the Soleil d'Or, he sat out at a little table on the pavement, in his red fez, and drank tea, but he ate nothing. His legs were swollen and causing him some trouble. I sat with him for a time and he talked about the possibility of going to Geneva, etc, but nothing was decided then.

We went up to the caves, reaching them with some difficulty. G.'s car would not take the slope, so he transferred

---

[1] Not only the tape-worm.

to the Vauxhall and Mr. B. drove him to the very entrance. M. Windels was there, and took us round; Ravidat and Marsal and the dogs: they all remembered us from last year.

Gurdjieff was evidently anxious to see the caves. It was lovely to be there with him - I remember him standing with his feet apart, leaning on his stick, with his head thrown back, looking up at the great stag with the stylized antlers in the first gallery. I was left at the end of the party to close the iron doors, but I sneaked up afterwards and came close behind him to hear what he said. Even then I could not hear it all. He said that the composite animal is an "*emblem*". "A symbol?" said Mr. B., and he replied, "No, an *emblem* like the Sphinx." He was much interested in it. He said the horns on the reindeer are like Beelzebub's horns, representing the degree of attainment. The curious 'trap' drawings he said are "letters like the Chinese", and that each has a special meaning. He insisted that the paintings are only 8,000 years old, not as the experts say, 18 to 20 thousand. He insisted that this work was done *after* the loss of Atlantis. He also said that there must without fail be dolmens within 5 kilometres of the caves. If these dolmens could be found, he will study them and visit the caves again.

When we left the caves, the hired car party returned to Paris and Mr. G., choosing Lise, Iovanna and the two Mills for his car, told Mr. B., with Tim, Bernard and me, to return to Paris without him. We went with him to Tulle and there, after stopping at a café for some iced drinks, we left him. I don't know where he went.

So we went leisurely on. We stopped at the little village where old Madeleine lives. (There was a fair there). She sat on a bench at her door in the sun, a little tiny creature, 89 years old. She did not of course know who I was, but she kissed me on both cheeks and held my hand. We had a good lunch at Uzerche and went on to Bourges. We dined there and went up to the cathedral, which looked marvellous and unearthly in the light of one lamp and the stars.

September 2nd

J.G.B. 7.30 a.m. BOURGES Now I must try to reconstruct these last days. On Wednesday morning we started at 9 o'clock and drove through Clermont Ferrand over by the Puy de Dome to Mont Dore where we had a very grand lunch, ordered by me from Vichy.

We motored on through La Bourboule, Ursel and Tulle to Brive, stopping for sleep in the forest. G. seemed to enjoy his lunch very much. He has certainly taken on a difficult task with John M. and it is most instructive to watch the care with which he approaches it. He uses food in the most powerful way as a means of approaching people. We reached Montignac at 9 p.m. G. was very tired and had to drink coffee frequently to avoid going to sleep. Nevertheless we had dinner about 9.45 at the Soleil d'Or and sat over it until 11.30. He did not eat much, but praised the ice cream. He complained that his room was not comfortable and that he needed his own bathroom to give himself a treatment. He talked very little, but was particularly gentle and kind with the old woman who was waiting on us. Although at first inclined to be displeased with the simplicity of the fare, he saw how sincerely the Bourgs had tried to please him and was very kind to them both. After dinner I had a talk with E. in the garden of the hotel. I walked back with her at 1 a.m. to her lodging and we swam in the Vezere, I was sleeping at the other end of the town, and the others were dispersed in various places.

At 7 a.m. I went and saw to the cars and came back to the Soleil d'Or just before 8 to find G. already down for breakfast. We left for the caves a little after 9. Great trouble about getting his car up the gradient.

G. was very tired and his legs are evidently troubling him.

Nevertheless he came in my car to the top and after waiting for another party to go through we went down with Windels at about 10 a.m. There is no doubt that he was interested and impressed. He said that the cave drawings are certainly very old, about 8,000 years. He said that there should be without fail

7 dolmens within 5 kilometres of the caves. If those dolmens could be found, he would come and study them and then spend some time in the caves. He spoke about the horns of the deer as symbolizing the degree of attainment in the same way as the horns of Beelzebub. Indeed on looking at the disposal of the horns it was obvious that they were conventional and quite unlike the completely realistic oxen and horses. I asked him about some of the signs. He said they were letters like the Chinese, about 45 of them existed, each with a special meaning. He was very much interested in the "composite animal" at the entrance, and said this was an "emblem, like the Sphinx", and said that this was how it was in Atlantis. I remembered that he had written of the Sphinx as the emblem of the Society Akhaldan, and realized that he implied that we had here at Lascaux the centre of such a society and that this animal was its emblem and at the same time the reminding factor for its work.

When we left the caves he was buying photographs for everyone. There was an unmistakable appropriateness about his being there.

He seemed to be entirely at home there and everything was quiet and we stood round him very peaceful and happy. He did not say any more, except to tell Iovanna to send the pictures to her father and tell him that these paintings were very old and should be very interesting to him. She said she was most sorry that he was unable to be there.

As I was driving him down, I said that the prehistorians were agreed that these paintings were dated between 15,000 and 25,000 years back. G. said, no, not more than 8,000. I said there was evidence from the implements and bones. "It is thought", I said, "that they go back before the time of the loss of Atlantis." He immediately replied in a rather shocked tone, "How can that be? These cannot be before the loss of Atlantis". He then remained silent, and I could get no more out of him.

He was evidently working out a plan in his own mind, for as soon as we had all collected by the cars in front of the caves, he said, "Who go Paris?" and the two Nicholls, Mrs. von H. and Miss A. had been bundled almost unceremoniously off in the hired car. He selected the two Millses, Iovanna and Lise for his own car; this left Mrs. D., E.M., Bernard and me, expecting to follow him home. But as soon as he left the caves he began to make it clear that he did not want us, and finally without any ceremony, at Tulle, he said, "I go left; you go right." I said, "Then we must say goodbye to you", and he replied, "Yes; goodbye!" and that was that.

He drove off very fast as soon as he had drunk some iced Vitelloise. We turned north and came through Uzerche, where we had lunch and reached Bourges at 8.45. After dinner we walked up and saw the cathedral, faintly lighted.

We went to bed at 11. I did my task from 11.15 till 12.15. How I shall drive myself out of this Paradise to earn my spiritual bread again by the sweat of my brow I do not know. I do know that this is a supreme test. If I can do it, I shall get the completion of my second body. If not, I shall be a very wretched creature.

In the morning we visited the cathedral and got permission to go round the triforium and clerestory and to visit the façade and the roof. From Bourges we went to Fontainebleau. I showed Mrs. D. the Prieuré and then we had a picnic in the forest. We had much trouble with the car all day as the radiator is choked. We did not reach Paris till after 5, so I went straight to the Gare du Nord, having dropped the others, to meet Polly, George and Mary. It turned out that they had arrived by air the day before, so I visited them at the Chevreuse. I spent the evening with them and went out in the car with P. to the Bois. We stood for a long time watching the moon set across the Seine. Polly is much better than she was a month ago.

E.B. We returned to Paris via Fontainebleau, where we had a picnic in the forest. In Paris we found that Mr. G. will not be here till tomorrow.

September 3rd

J.G.B. *1.30 a.m.* Back in Paris. I have watched and watched all the time in order to observe my own state. The need all the time to do what one does not want and to deny oneself the things that one does want is all part of the work of establishing the second body. But that is not all: it is at least as important to 1) remain for an hour or more daily in the collected state so that crystallization can proceed and 2) to practise many, many times a day the transfer of consciousness from the first to the second body. Can one renounce Paradise and at once occupy oneself with the greater work of Purgatory? After the happiness and enjoyment at the last four days, I may be tempted.

8 a.m. It is quite easy to suffer up to a point, but all the time there are doubtful moments - "Need I do this?" I know how precarious is my hold on that separation.

6 p.m. It all came up suddenly as G. was speaking of yesterday and saying that he could not eat because he was used to company and he had had only four people with him. I said that he had sent us away. Then he turned on me and said that I had told him that I had to go and fetch my wife, but she had been here all the time. I had not been honest. My manifestations during the last week had been disgusting. At that point the toast of the Round Idiots came and when I said "to my health also", he said, "You not round. You know and yet you manifest so. During the last week I hate your manifestations."

I did not feel either outwardly or inwardly affected by his vehemence. His eyes blazed at me and yet I could feel his inner calm and also my own. But, of course, I asked myself if I have misunderstood him entirely.

At lunch he thundered against the English and their failures in the past. Yet we all know that the English have been his most staunch and generous supporters. Even so, we cannot help feeling what he says. How can I tell? Did he enjoin upon me such a difficult life with no respite at all? If so, it would mean that I had quite misunderstood him during the last 7 days. In the last resort, I must know myself. I shall find out when I return to England and the problem of adapting myself to all the conditions of life there.

As the day went on I have been filled more and more with sadness. In the evening I spoke to Mme. de S. about G.'s tirade

SEPTEMBER 4TH

at lunch, and asked her help. She was very serious about it and said that it might refer to some mishandling of G.'s plans. For example, I had suggested that B. should go on the trip. This had encouraged others to go by train, etc. I told Mme. de S. that I had really quite misunderstood him. I also said that until he spoke at lunch I had felt no remorse of conscience, and this really distressed me, because if I had done wrong I ought to have known it. She did not say much, but left it the more emphatic by saying nothing!

We went to the apartment, where there were about 50 people. I read the end of the '5th Descent' and 'Ashiata Shiemash' up to the end of the Legominism. Gurdjieff came in half way through, having spoken for some time to Mme. de S. in his little room. I could feel the difference in his attitude towards me. This was confirmed in several ways during dinner.

He made E.M. do the Addition with the supplement, "or even sometimes like rabid dogs" about which he had spoken at lunch time. Then he made her give the whole toast in French with the Addition, and said, "Bravo, Elizabeth. Now I give you diplome for French language. I make you *secretar* to some ministre. But he not ministre yet - perhaps in one or two years." He also made a fuss of me over my toast. I knew that Mme. de S. had spoken to him and he had been convinced that I had sincerely misunderstood him.

But it is difficult to bear. I rebuke myself and think of the greatness of the task which lies before me and ask how it is possible that I cannot liberate myself from this weakness in myself. But of course I know the necessity of this task. I know that I must establish that I AM which can listen always to the voice of God. That can only come by being alone for a long time.

E.B. Mr. G. came back in time for lunch. We were a large crowd. I was in my corner. He shouted at Mr. B. and told him that he is not a Round Idiot, "because you *know* and yet you manifest so". Unlike Page, he said.

At dinner he made me give the Addition with at the end

of it, "Sometimes even like rabid dogs", as he had explained at lunch. Then he made me repeat the addition and the toast in French. I knew that this was important and got frightened: in any case I was in a state of nerves. But at the end he said, "Bravo, Yelizabet. I will give you diploma for French language. Now I can make you *secretar* some ministre. But not yet - he not ministre yet. Perhaps one year - two years."

September 4th

J.G.B. Many times G. has spoken about the necessity to redescend consciously - that is, to throw away what one has already gained and begin a fresh struggle towards Being. How great an abyss there is between the words and the reality! Our minds accept with stupid alacrity all kinds of great sacrifices and labours. But when we have to experience them we know a new world, and wonder, who can live in it? G. spoke the other day about hell and said, "It is only terrible for the first few days." But I cannot see how I can suffer as I am suffering now without hope of deliverance. But I know only too well that this will pass and I shall settle down to the new conditions ...

But I should have seen deeper. Had I been able to do that, and continue my previous line in spite of G.'s encouragement to depart from it (with his talk of Paradise, and all that), I should by now be truly free. I can see that I have failed to make a very big step. But what insight that would have required!

11 a.m. I have been with Mr. G. for 1½ hours at the café. I met him while starting the car outside No. 6. At the café he would not let me sit at his table, but said in an angry voice, "People come and sit here and waste my time and then I lose my clients. They do not come because they think I am occupied." For about half an hour he put a barrier of hostility up against me. Then I asked some practical questions about money matters, to which he replied shortly. He spoke of curing someone and "putting him on feet" and the obligation of his mother to pay heavily for this.

After a few minutes' silence I asked if he would see Polly here or at the flat. He said at the flat at 1.15. I then said I thanked him for what he was doing for her. I added, "I cannot thank you for what you have done for me. That I can never repay."

A long time passed during which various people came and spoke to him. Then he turned to me and said slowly, "What you say about never repay - this stupidity. *Only* you can repay. What do you think is money? I can buy all your England. Only *you*" (with great emphasis) "can repay me with work. But what do you do? Before trip I give you task. Do you fulfill? No, you do opposite. Never once I see you *lutter*[1] with yourself. You are all times occupied with your cheap animal." He spoke very simply and quietly and was going to say more when one of his patients came in. I got up to go and he said, "Go for walk and then come back".

I went round to tell Polly about seeing him.

When I returned he told me that the man who had come had been a paralytic whom he had cured and "put on feet". He had just paid him 50,000 francs, which he showed me. "How he get I don't know. Very difficult for Russe. But he get." Then he added with a very kind smile, "I think this have some connection with our conversation. I two nights not sleep because of you. Now you must repay."

As I sat silent in the café wrestling with my problems I felt my strength returning and knew once again that definite sensation in my neck and thorax which is the physical side of the 'second life'. I said to him that I was very stupid and trusted in my own mind. I could not help to avoid such bad things unless I could always have conscience awake. He did not reply. Soon after he got up and drove away, saying, "Let wife come 1.15. All come half past one."

5 p.m. It is exactly a month to the hour since I arrived in Paris and I leave with a more tranquil heart and greater hope than I thought possible even a few hours ago. As I went with G. to his car from the café this morning, I said, "How can conscience awaken? Only by this can such things be avoided." He did not reply then, but when lunch came he spoke several times. It so happened that we were reading Ashiata Shiemash, <u>which struck the</u> whole core of the matter.

1 Struggle.

At lunch he suddenly turned to me and said, "You think I not hear your question. About what else we speak all the week?" He said that conscience can only be brought into consciousness by the intensity of our inner struggle. When I said goodbye to him he spoke to me in Russian and for the first time used the 'thou' of intimacy. So in three words he brought me close to him again.

Meanwhile, I had left the flat to drive Mme. de S. back to her house. She said that the work changes. Up to one point one has fairly clear guidance. Then it is made so confusing that one can easily do exactly the wrong thing in the conviction that one is doing right. Anyhow, I know that my time has not been wasted. I go with remorse of conscience in my heart rather than a feeling of achievement. I see very well how I have exaggerated and how this led to my downfall. The subtlety of Gurdjieff's teaching goes beyond what one can imagine! Everything within me is so wonderfully well that I could wish to die at this moment. I feel inwardly free from all the heavy stupidity which has come away like a loathsome vomit, leaving one clean and refreshed inside. My second life beats ten times more strongly than before - only a few hours after I was terrified that I had strangled it at birth! Moreover I have learned the secret of the double inner work. I will struggle to do it, with Gurdjieff's help.[1]

E.B. It is now clear that Mr. G. thought that J.G.B. was acting deliberately, not having made a mistake. How neatly he walked into the trap! I have heard about the conversation in the café this morning. The Bennetts left at 8.30 p.m. I drove them to Le Bourget.

At lunch Mr. G., noticing Marie-Claude sitting in the fireplace, beautiful as ever in a new mauve dress, said how much she helps him: he goes to a cinema when he wants to rest, looks at the screen when he wants to sleep, and Claude has the same effect on him as a cinema. But, he said, she is stupid; she does not make any charge for this!

---

[1]   J.G.B. did not continue his diary after his return to London that day.

A propos something or other, Page told him the story of "We shall light this day such a candle as shall never be put out", and G. said, at once, yes; but was that candle in fact still burning?

Fourteen new arrivals, with Miss Heap at their head, arrived this evening. There were 45 or more at dinner and I was not in the dining room at all. Rina was called in as *Egout pour Sweet*, and I for the Addition, but otherwise we were not within earshot. Adie was Director.

September 5th

At dinner, Gurdjieff spoke while he was eating, and made himself cough. He said that the "*ancien regle* was good", and told us how at the Prieuré no one spoke in the dining room - "afterwards go out, smoke, speak - only not in dining room".

He was, both at lunch and dinner, very kind to me today. Only the odd word, or look, or bowl of *salade* or something, but I was grateful. Usually in his presence one suffers more, but these last few days my only relief has been in his presence.

Scylla, newly arrived, sat opposite to him, and he was much intrigued and said that he had seen her before, or perhaps her mother or grandmother, in the Jewish quarter of Odessa, or Rovno, or a town I had never heard of with a name that sounded like 'Perdition'. He reverted several times to this, and watched her very intently. Later he rather implied, as he did when she was here before, that she is a Swaggering Idiot, but she herself chose Compassionate.

At 8.45 this morning, Rina and I went to the flat to do the previous night's washing up, with Emil.

September 6th

I felt very ill yesterday, and this morning woke with a sore throat and a bad headache. I went back to bed and did not go to the flat the whole day - the first time I have voluntarily missed a chance. I am grateful for a day of quiet. There is so much to think about. There is so much to be learnt, if only I can both clasp it to myself and also contrive to keep it at arm's length.

Rina came to see me when she returned from the flat tonight, about 2.30. She was reminding me of the conversation some time ago (20.8.) when G. spoke about the bank only for those who could write a cheque for 6 *zéros*. In this he was talking about levels of man, and saying that he is Man No. 7, and that only those can work in his school who are man No. 6. She said that tonight he was in tremendously good form and very amusing, and they had all spent most of the evening in fits of laughter. He told about how he always carries sweets for children and sugar for dogs, and how this is "small secret". And the story of "Cow looking on new *peinte porte*". Many other stories, but few of them bear repetition, except from Mr. G.

His Armenian masseur has returned now, and says that his legs will be all right in a week, but that it is quite time they had some attention. Mme. de S. says that now he feels the benefit of the trip, and how good it is for him to have new impressions and also to exercise his body, in driving, etc.

September 7th

The greater part of my time here is past. Have I still any chance to retrieve myself?

I went to the flat for lunch. Page read - we finished 'Material Questions'. We seem to have embarked on a complete reading of the Second Series, but doubtless we shall not reach the end uninterrupted. The party has thinned out it little in the last few days; we are now somewhere between 35 and 40.

Mr. G., in contrast to his behaviour on Monday, was completely withdrawn today. Sometimes he does not speak to me or noticeably look at me and yet I know that he is perfectly aware of me and amiably disposed. At other times he can make you feel his complete indifference, and yet again he can actually withdraw behind a barrier. This he did with me today. As I waited inside the dining room door for the *chaine*, he said in an irritated sort of voice, "Yelizabet, you know your place: sit, quickly, quickly!" which I did. From then on he took no notice of me. He was looking at me at the 4th toast, but did not ask for the addition. Once or twice during the meal he looked at me with no feeling or expression whatever in his eyes - complete withdrawal. Then at the end he roared at me for not drinking honourably. This did not disturb me in the least inwardly. Indeed, I don't know why it should: I had decided in advance to drink only half the established quantity and had done it blatantly, expecting some such upheaval at the end.

But when nearly everyone had gone from the dining room and I was clearing the table, he suddenly said, standing by his chair, hitching up his trousers, "Yelizabet! Now we go in other room, coffee drink", in an amiable voice. So for once I went in, and drank coffee, and heard his recording and the replay.

At night I felt very ill and had a temperature and yet didn't want to miss anything: I went to the reading (My Father), helped in the *chaine* _ without going into the dining room, and then, having told Mme. de S., went home. I wanted to stay, but I know I couldn't have played my rôle. Tomorrow I will hear what was said.

September 8th

I forgot to write two things he said at lunch yesterday. One - Round Idiots - "I *love* such Idiot" and, "but Mr. Gurdjieff, I am Round Idiot. Then necessary everything forgive". And, "I notice what never Round Idiot choose Round Idiot. This very clever choose."

Then, suddenly, out of the blue, "Where is Doctor?" (Bernard has been gone for several days). "He has left". "With whom he go?" "With Mr. Adie". "Ah. Good combination." He was silent for a moment, smiling to himself, and then, "Mr. Bennett, Mrs. Bennett, Doctor - they good companions. But Doctor, better than cinema!"

At lunch today, Mr. G. asked for my spoon and filled it with delicious hot *salade*. Otherwise he took no notice of me, but did not cut me off from him.

Iovanna left during the music, to go back to Chicago. Mme. Duprez and I went with her to the Gare des lnvalides. She cried most of the time behind large dark glasses. When she had left, Mme. Duprez suggested that I should go shopping with her, so we rolled away in her big black Cadillac to a precious-stone place in the Rue du Châteaudun to buy a stone for an icon she has found for Mr. G. Then on to a dog shop for travelling baskets for her dog and cat. We talked about the work and the conditions in which one works, about her husband, about Eve, about one's attitude to Mr. G. It was good that we could speak at once of these things, although we had never exchanged a word before.

In the evening we read 'My First Tutor' and started 'Pogossian'. Mr. Gurdjieff said little at dinner - in fact the first part of the meal was eaten in total silence - but the atmosphere was particularly good, I thought. He asked for the addition, and tonight I really felt what I was saying ..

September 9th

Liliane was there tonight, without her husband. He made a great fuss of her, and was very amusing all through the meal. The Kings and Joneses and Henry B. were all newly arrived. G. told the story of the English, and various others that I have heard before. He remembered Mrs. King, and called her "Mother". He talked to Mr. King about *zéros*. At the end, when I was clearing the table, he said to me, "You saw, Yelizabet, what I prepare a *candidat* for shearing?" "Yes, Monsieur, I saw". "You understand what I speak about *zéros*?" "Yes". "Then you are very intelligent if understand this", and he went on to say that for shearing the preparation is the most important thing; if that is done carefully, when the time comes the wool just falls off He had talked at dinner about the increasing scarcity of wool in England, and how soon he must turn his attention to America.

We read 'Yeloff'.

I was Verseur at lunch, and in my corner for dinner. I spent a happy morning in the Musée de l'Homme. Usually I don't get beyond the Old Man of Cromagnon, but this morning I went quickly through it all and came back at the end to the Old Man.

September 10th

We read 'Lubovedski' as far as the beginning of Solovieff.

SEPTEMBER 10TH

Gurdjieff made an addition to the cow story at lunch: how the cow and calf went to and fro through the forest all night, and when in the morning the patron found they were missing, "he beginnen be nervous", and went to the door and found them asleep outside, worn out. So he had pity on her, and sent them off as usual to "pass day in forest".

He made me, in my corner, Bouche d'egout, and passed me half a kidney and a fresh sliced tomato to eat - delicious. There were many Square Idiots today, and he teased us about being "cheap merchandise". He passed a huge wedge of melon to John Mills, standing in the doorway, and then began to cough. Eat it quickly, he said, between bursts of coughing, so that I can finish coughing.

He scolded one of Miss Heap's group for not having chosen an Idiot, after being here six days, and the girl said she didn't know which to choose - always she wanted to choose a different one. He did not like this, and said this was "dishonest" in her, and such uncertainty was a sure sign "what you are not honest".

I met several of the Heaps for coffee this morning, and was glad to have some sort of contact with them. I think I have spoken to them all now except two, which is an advance for me! Miss Heap, too; I have never spoken to her till this week.

This evening I was Director. I was very nervous, for some reason, and did not feel at all happy till my second glass of vodka. I did the whole thing very badly, and came away feeling entirely dissatisfied. I don't know what went wrong, really; I behaved outwardly correctly and did not muddle the plates or forget the toasts or neglect Mr. G. in any way; I just never felt happy about it.

He spoke about Hopeless Idiots - this was the high spot of the evening. He said that the trouble was that hardly anyone has an aim of any sort. A few people have the aim to help Our Endlessness, but this is a very great aim, not for everyone. But everyone can come to such an aim if they will start by having an aim "only not die like dog, but die honorable". Everyone can understand this, he said. If everyone will take this aim -

or indeed, any aim - for one month, they will find that this will make their whole life different. "And truth", he said, looking into my eyes with a smile of the greatest kindness and understanding, "truth, this life can sometimes be good, objectively". He often closes a serious discussion with a joke: he did today. Very few people in Europe have an aim, he said. The French, yes, and the English - "English have aim eat always - gam and eggs: French have aim eat - *soupe à l'onion, avec onion*", and so it all ended in laughter.

September 11th

We read the part of 'Lubovedski' today about his - the Prince's - meeting with the old Tamil at the house of the Aga Khan, and the wonderful speech about "the desire of your mind being the desire of your heart". I have heard that again and again since I came, and each time I hear it differently, perhaps understanding a little more, perhaps becoming aware of a whole new aspect which I do not understand at all, and never even suspected. It is so for me with all the Second Series.

September 14th

Lees's[1] birthday. All sorts of things have happened in the last few days. On Sunday someone came unexpectedly for lunch who had not seen Mr. G. since 30 years in Constantinople, a Russian, I think. He had heard quite by chance of Mr. G.'s presence in Paris and arrived to see him at 3 p.m., when lunch was fairly advanced. He reminded Mr. G. of former acquaintances and happenings, and it was extraordinary to see that Mr. G. would not in any way respond to all this: he simply did not react. He was very hospitable, as he always is, and even obviously pleased to see this man: he simply would not talk to him about the past. The man talked incessantly, but when he spoke of Constantinople, Mr. G. went on quietly eating, without looking at him, appearing not to listen, and each time, after a few minutes, he quietly brought back the conversation to the present moment, to the room and the people in it. The

---

1 [Elizabeth's elder brother. Ed.]

SEPTEMBER 14TH

visitor was, I think, quite unaware of this, and talked very entertainingly. I left early to drive Mme. de S., so I did not see how it ended.

He has shown great kindness to the Kings, calling them "Father" and "Mother", giving them various special foods, etc. They have very often been *Egout*, or rather he has, with Mrs. King sitting beside him. But one day, after talking about their relationship, he said that for Mr. King, his dependence on his wife was "a very great sin, this weakness".

One day Scylla asked if she could change her Idiot, but G. said no - or at least, no unless she is prepared to "pay his spend for one day". In order to find out how much that is, she must ask his secretary, etc. But he has twice given her clear indications that she is Swaggering Idiot. Remembering the two occasions on which he said this, and remembering the whole scene when she asked if she could change, I am able to see something new. If she had said, "I want to change to Swaggering Idiot", instead of saying, "Please may I change my Idiot?" the whole outcome would have been different.

We finished the Second Series, contrary to my expectations, without interruption, and are embarked now on the Prologue to the Third Series. G. makes John M. read very often now. The whole of his treatment of John is fascinating to watch. Marianne says she has not seen him treat anyone in this way, either here or in America, with such gentleness and care. Actually I don't think she is right in this, from what I have seen: I think he pays even so much attention to many of us - even to M. herself - but we just don't notice. But with John the effect is very striking. In one fortnight he is a different creature, both in his general behaviour and in his behaviour to me personally. Mr. G. made some comment on all this at dinner tonight. He sent John out to the kitchen to fetch something and when he had gone he looked after him, smiling, and said, "What change, hein?"

M. was tired and did not. come tonight (it didn't matter from the point of view of the Director, because Lemaître was there), but G. asked where she was and said, "She is young, but she is very often tired," in a curious voice, but no other comment.

At lunch there was a wonderful conversation about parents and children, making a place for God, etc. I could not write it down, even if I could remember it all; it wasn't that sort of conversation. G. has also spoken again about this "small aim" not to perish like a dog. About how "even now it is not too late - even today," even for an old man. Only old people have less time than the young: naturally for them it is "more *dur*", they must work harder.

September 16th

I am writing this on a very rough crossing between Dieppe and Newhaven. Everyone is being sick, and we will be at least three quarters of an hour late. They have battened us in with horrible canvas screens, but when you go aft you can see the water, all green and grey and yellow, with huge frilly waves. Below, one is plunged every moment or two into shadow as a wave breaks against the port hole, and then the drops run down the glass, evenly, like fat when you tilt the frying pan. I left Paris at 2.30 this morning. Oh, dear, someone has just been so sick beside me. But I suppose it might have been in my lap. I enjoyed my drive, and being alone. In Dieppe I went and sat for a long time in the church of St. Jacques, and tried to separate yesterday from tomorrow. Everything went wrong in Dieppe. I hadn't slept, of course, and I had to have half my petrol pumped out of the tank, and a man in the queue told me, in front of a lot of other people, that I was dishonest - all the things that would have made me peevish not so long ago.

A little thing I have remembered, rather late. In the days immediately following the trip to Lascaux, I had no opportunity to thank Mr. G. for it, and after that I was too totally miserable and at sea to be able to speak to him, but I finally said one day, "Thank you for taking me on the trip last week". He was sitting in his chair, after the music, and I knelt on the floor beside him. He turned and looked at me. "Why you thank me?" . "Because I learnt something useful. I learnt that hell can be as profitable as paradise." He smiled. "Not thank me for this today". "Why not?" "Wait one day, then thank me." I did not understand, but I said, "All right. But I still thank you today as well", and I kissed his cheek and went away.

September 23rd

I was happy today because I was going back to Paris. I went with Mr. B. on the Golden Arrow. The crossing was perfectly smooth. We had lunch on the train, and when we reached Paris we sat for an hour in a café opposite the Gare du Nord. We talked about many things. There is quite a large party of 'our' people here, Rita, Katya, Rina, Nigella, Julian and Edgar.

But at the reading (in G.'s bedroom; it was French night), we were only nine English. Page read 'From the Author' and 'The Arch Preposterous'. There wasn't a very big crowd at dinner. I found a seat in the fireplace. I thought Gurdjieff-looked extraordinarily well, much better than I expected after all the news I heard in England. I did not make any sort of connection with him. Lemaître was Director, and at Hopeless Idiots Mr. G. looked directly at me, but as though he did not really recognize me. He needed an addition, and I think if I had been in my corner he would have asked for it. As it was, he stressed the distinction between the two kinds, and left it. Mr. B. - Egout - knocked Mr. G.'s melon on to the floor, and Mr. G. said amiably, "This brouve what you are Round Idiot", as the toast came immediately afterwards.

He seemed rather bored with us all.

September 24th

I had breakfast at the Chevreuse with Mr. B. H.T. made his first appearance at lunch, and it was a great success. It was one of those really marvellous meals, which are quite impossible to describe. H.T. responded in just the right way. He understood pretty well, talked and listened and had an extraordinarily good feeling about it all. What a nice man.

Mr. G. was explaining how men and women, old men and children, must divide their glasses of alcohol, but "sometimes

I forget, and drink more". H.T. said, in an aside, "What is he drinking, anyway? Coca Cola?" Mr. G. heard, of course, and immediately had H.'s red vodka removed and gave him instead a full glass of Armagnac from his own bottle, leaving the bottle beside him.

When the camel sausage came round, H. said, "How do you mean, camel?" and Rita said, "Well, *camel*", "Yes, but where do they *get* the camel?", which, I must confess, has long been a question on which I dare not dwell.

Gurdjieff asked for the addition, and afterwards gave caviare to Mme. de S. and then to me, and to Rita, H.T., etc. H.T. asked about Krishnamurti, and Mr. G. talked about Mrs. Besant, Mme. Blavatsky etc. He said he had met B. When H.T. asked about her brother, now dead, Mr. G. said, "ask her", nodding at me. So I said the brother died like a dirty dog. He went on to talk about India: how many people go there looking for truth, but India is only "*bordel* for truth".

I can't remember it all, and it is anyway impossible to write it all down. So much depends on the moment, and G.'s voice, expression, etc.

When, à propos something or other, he said to Mr. B. something about Shakespeare having been a passive pederast, H.T. turned incredulously to Rita. "Did he say pederast?" "Shakespeare", said Rita economically, and H.T. said with relief, "Oh, *Shakespeare!*" and we all laughed very much.

There were so many little small things. I expect they will be coming back to me for days. H. T. was entranced. He turned again and again to Mme. de S. or Rita, and said, "What a man!" and how he had never seen "a human being with a smile like that", and "he is as naughty as he could be, but he is still irresistible", etc. And Mr. G. said to Mme. de S. that already H.T. was beginning to be sympathetic and "I like him", with another engaging smile. He was really at his best: H. provided just the right sort of stimulus.

Afterwards was Mme. de S.'s movements at 7. Very few of us: only eight people working, and an audience of seven!

In the evening we finished the Prologue, which we had

been reading at lunch, and which seems so exactly to answer some of my immediate problems. We were not many, about 20. All the places in the dining room were filled, but it was not overcrowded. I sat at the small table with Sophia, Julian and Alfred. Page was in the corner by the piano. I could hear practically nothing. I could not see Mr. G., either, except in the looking glass on the sideboard, so at the end I stood up. We went as far as Doubting Idiots·.

Mr. G. had a long conversation in Russian with Katya, who was arguing that God is in some way responsible for the state of deadlock of Enlightened Idiots. (I could not understand the Russian, but Mr. B. told me afterwards.) G. said that what Katya said was entirely wrong: how could God be responsible for every microbe in every drop of water? The state of the Enlightened Idiot depended on the conditions at the moment of conception, etc.

He spoke about the necessity of playing a rôle without inner "identification. He played a very long music afterwards.

There was a long conversation about fish, and about Nigella's name, and G. connected her in some way with K.P. - something about having the same sort of swaggering, or something. But I could hardly hear at all. He took a long time over making the *salade*, and there was no conversation at first. The atmosphere felt very good - in fact for me it was a 'good evening', in spite of the difficulties of hearing and seeing, etc.

The swelling of his feet has quite subsided, but he is coughing more than he was when I went away. I was amused to hear H.T. ask Rita, "What is his hearing like?" I am rather inclined to take for granted that his hearing is perfect, and forget how very extraordinary it is in a man who "have already eighty three years".

September 25th

Katya came to my room this morning and reconstructed last night's conversation for me. She remembers very completely and accurately what G. says, and also has no difficulty in understanding him. It is good to see her so happy and relaxed.

Later I went to the café with the whole of our party, and T.

At lunch we did not get far with the reading, as G. came in and brought it to an end at 2 o'clock. Mr. B. said, the reading is very interesting, but of course we will do as you wish, and G. said eating also was very interesting, so we all trooped into the dining room. By the way, H.T. asked G. what he thought about Gandhi, and Mr. G. said he did not know, but it was very significant that they had killed him. Until they killed him, he wasn't sure.

He spoke to E.C. about his idiot, and how from this moment everything that goes well for him will be due to Mr. G. having drunk his health today, and that E.C. must give him nine *pour cent*. (E.'s 'uncle' - the bishop - was invented on the spur of the moment by Mr. B., as a sort of justification of E.'s 'arch idiot'.)

I went into the room for the music, and tonight as well: it did produce in me a great determination to work. During the reading of the Introduction to Third Series in the evening, Mr. G. came in at 11.15, and I was afraid he would stop us, but he let us go on reading till Lise came in and said it was already midnight. I think we were all surprised to find how late it was.

He seemed rather bored with us at dinner, and disinclined to talk.

Page was in the corner, and I sat next to M., who was Verseur. We weren't many, about 20, I suppose. We were all in the dining room. Only near the end of the meal he turned to Mr. B. and spoke about Lise; how she is universal, she can fill any place. If Sophia is not there, "*au diable avec elle*", Lise will record the music, etc. If he told her to play the rôle of President of the United States, "from now three hours" she will do this. He said this was easier for her because she began to learn when she was only eleven. He called her in and asked her when she had first met him, and she replied that it was when she was eleven, at a Christmas party for the children. He went on to say that she could even play the part of Mme. de S.

We left the flat soon after 2, and Mr. B. and I walked down the Champs Elysées to the Deauville care, where we talked over the occurrences of the day. I went to bed about 3.30. I feel in a curious state of suspension, or lull, since I returned to Paris. I think this is dangerous, and today I shall do all I can to break out of it.

September 26th

Last night Mr. G. told E.C. that he looked like an old Jew on his name's day! I went to the café this morning with Rina, Nigella and Julian.

At lunch we went on with the Introduction. Mr. G. came in near the beginning, but was called away by Lise ten minutes before the end. When he returned, stopping, as he often does, in the doorway and saying, "Director! I think, enough", he turned to Mme. de S. and said that he had never heard that chapter read so well. He said to Mr. B., "What happens with you?" and to Mme. de S., if only they had such a reader in America. He was much pleased, and told Mr. B. that for this he must eat four times more!

The whole meal was roses, roses for Mr. B. He was fussed over and complimented and given food in a way that ordinarily one could only regard as sinister, but somehow this time it felt sincere, not a trap or a sarcasm. Mr. G. made one good pun. T. asked him if it was known how many people eat there in a year - how many different people. He replied, no, it wasn't known: people go, come - only unchangeable I! The meal was not a long one, and Mr. B. left before the music for Le Bourget, and me with him. We both had rather the feeling of the last moments of a holiday.

There were movements from 7 till 9. Salle 32 is being repainted, so we were in 81, very cramped and airless. Fortunately we were only 20, but even so we could not do any of the large "*tableau*" movements. It was very hot - even Mme. de S., at the piano, was mopping her brow! I was very tired afterwards, physically, which is unusual, with a really bad back ache and none of the usual feeling of renewed energy. Apparently many people felt the same. Solange, too; she said she also was very tired. I had a drink with E.C. and afterwards a bath[1] in his bathroom, and was somewhat restored by 10.30, when we went to the flat.

Page read, and we finished the Introduction. It finishes in mid-air, as the last pages are either missing or not written. Mr. G. was annoyed about that, as he was enjoying the reading, and had rather an inquest on it in Russian with Mme. de S. Page joined in with the complaint that it was difficult to make sense of it as it was translated word for word from the Russian (a remark that I once made to Mme. de S., after struggling with the reading, with the same result), but she said it was meant to be like that, and would not be worked over again.

Dinner was exciting for what he said about Hopeless Idiots. If you want to perish like a dog - well ... But if you wish die *honorable*, wish not wish, you must work on yourself.

Mr. G. had a lot of Russian conversation with Katya, who answered back briskly, and, I thought, once too often, because there was one moment when he obviously wanted to close the discussion and she went on. But I gathered it was all like last night, telling her she isn't Russian at all - in fact, he actually said, in English, "She is Russian like his Uncle", nodding at E.C.

By the end of the evening I was phenomenally tired and left as soon as the table was cleared, as soon as he started playing. It was early, not yet one o'clock. Oh, yes, and about Hopeless Idiots he said we must struggle with the whole of ourselves to want to die honourably, it wasn't enough just to want it now and then, with parts of us: it is necessary to want this through and through.

September 27th

Last night, when Gurdjieff had finished talking about Hopeless Idiots and when we had actually drunk the toast, he said that tonight we were very few, but these few must be thankful that they were here, because they had heard this. (What he had been saying about work). Of all the millions of people who exist, it is they, these few, who have heard these words and should consider themselves lucky. These are not, of

---

1 There was no bath at the Hotel Rena.

SEPTEMBER 27TH

course, his words, but he said that we should be thankful, and said it more than once.

I had a busy time at lunch today. We were still very few, and I had to read - Lubovedski. We read till 2.30 and got as far as the part about Philos, at the beginning of Solovieff. Marthe did not come, so I did her job, and was given, with unusual ceremony, a large piece of aubergine. He said, "Yelizabet! Your big spoon", and took it gravely from me; he filled it with aubergine and returned it to me, watching me very intently. Sophia was not there and Lise was out, getting her visa for America, so when Gurdjieff asked for music, Marianne said she and I could do it. He seemed somewhat surprised at this, but agreed that we could try. He said, "if something happens", we could have his melon and grapes, but "if not something happens ... " I said hastily, "Don't let's talk about that," but he smiled amiably and continued, "not will have". As soon as I was free I went out and prepared the machine, and M. and I got successfully through one "music" - not recording, of course; only playing an old one. He said, "Bravo, Marianna and Yelizabet," and that if we would spend one half day with Mme. de Salzmann in her apartment, she should explain to us how to distinguish one clef from another! The second music went well enough, though M. whispered to me that G. was not enjoying it; he was, she said, tense and afraid we would break the machine. And indeed at the end I spoilt it; I switched off without a long enough pause, which always annoys him. He said we had cut it off before the music was finished, which was not in fact so, but it was a silly mistake and I should have known better.

At lunch when E.C.'s name was called, he said, "Ah, Biscope", with a wicked smile. He likes that joke.

I don't know what all this was about, except that I was in what we call "a good state" all day, and able to shake off the lethargy of the last few days.

At 7 we had a movements practice with Solange.

It was French night, and the half dozen or so English read, in G.'s room, from the only so far existing copy of "Fragments", starting at the beginning. Gurdjieff came in at ten and sat with us during the reading of the part about the carpet-selling.

There were not as many French as usual, and, with some crowding round the door, everyone got into the dining room. G. said little: some conversation in Russian with Mme. de S., some talk about *zéros* with Mrs. Pearce. He made Marianne give the toasts in both French and English, and I the addition in both languages. (Lemaître left after the reading). I sat just inside the door and ran to and fro to the kitchen.

One of the best bits of the evening came before the reading started, when we were just arrived. There were in his room Rina, Rita, Katya and myself. Mme. de S. came in, and Katya said, "After lunch Mr. Gurdjieff told us that we should spend half a day with you, so that you could tell us about the different keys of his music". Mme. de S. threw up her hands with a shout of laughter, saying, "Heaven forbid! I have not time, and anyway it is impossible". Then she became more serious, and sitting down in his armchair, she said, "But I will tell you one very interesting thing. I was not told this. I know this because I found it out for myself - Mr. Gurdjieff did not explain it to me". She went on to say how "this is all here", tapping the copy of Fragments, which she held between her hands; how if we read and understand the chapter on the Law of Seven, we will understand also about his music. It is all concerned with the octave. By "clef" he does not mean what is meant in ordinary music. This has great significance for him, and the movements also are based on this same octave. Sophia knows a lot about ordinary music, but she does not understand the Law of Octaves, so when he tells her to play two pieces of music, each in a different key, she sometimes fails to do what he wants, and he tells her that it is the same key, and to him it is, though to her understanding it is quite different. Mme. de S. said that in all the years she has listened to his music and all the years that she had studied, she had understood about this, but she had worked and learnt it for herself, without explanations from other people. So, she said, it was much more useful.

It was a fascinating talk, and I was glad that Katya asked about it.

September 28th

Marianne left today to return to the States.
We had no reading, as Mr. G., Mme. de S. and Sophia were having a music session when we arrived, so we waited in the passage till 2 and then went straight in to lunch when the music was over. Therefore Marianne, who had intended to arrive just in time for lunch, was too late, and I was already ensconced as Director when she came. I asked Mr. G. if I should change with her, but he said no. I was sorry, but I expect it was really a good thing. We were only about a dozen. G. said very little, nearly all about the "*château*", Apparently the present tenant goes on Friday, and G. talks of dining there that day. He said he was not hungry, and he ate practically nothing except a baked potato with butter. He gave Marianne things to eat and things for her parents to eat, and told her when she left to kiss him here and then go quickly, because aeroplane will not wait.

After lunch Rina and I drank coffee with Dr. and Mme. Egg and then went to the cinema to see the Marx Brothers. (We laughed uproariously, but no one else did. I don't think the French like them much, or else they are Culture, and not to be laughed at).

In the morning I went to the flat to wash up, with Mrs. P. and M. Blondeau. Then I checked some of Rina's typing with Rita.

Tonight Rina read for the first time, and was astonished to find herself considering about it, although we were only so few and she is well used to reading in London. She said this made her read badly, but I did not think so.

It was one of those evenings when Mr. G. was rather bored with us. He had a conversation in Russian with Katya, who was there for the last time. He was saying that what she receives here is very expensive, and she must pay. She said, "If one has no money, then what?" "Then you must sell your pants". She repeated, "But who will buy them?" He did not answer, but went on to say how interesting it is that one can tell everything about a person from their pants. She repeated, "But who will buy them?" and he said, "First, I will buy them. And there is someone else who will buy them."

He produced with pride, both at lunch and dinner, a freak vegetable - he called it a "*courgette*" - which had grown taller than Lise! An amazing thing. I do wonder what he will do with it.

He had a long conversation with poor Mrs. P., telling her how badly he needs *zéros*.

At 12.15 Mme.de S. came in, and he was pleased to see her, and became more lively. The meal went on a long time, with a discussion about different currencies, between Mme. de S., himself and Page.

September 29th

This day was not particularly outstanding - not one of the extraordinary days that sometimes happens. At lunch we were only about ten. Rina read very well, 'Lubovedski'.

Katya left in the morning, but was back again by 7 o'clock, having been unable to bring herself to leave. At Dieppe she simply came back again.

Movements at 6, a practice with Solange, and from 7 till 9 with Mr. G. He was very fierce with us, and everything we did was wrong, until we did his favourite No. 17, the Multiplication. Obviously this has for him some quite special significance, and luckily we did it well tonight. He smiled and said if only we did all the movements like that ...

Lemaître was Director at dinner, and before it Page read 'Form and Sequence' and afterwards finished 'Lubovedski'. I think 'Form and Sequence' is a marvellous chapter, but Mr. G. seemed rather bored with it and nodded in his chair, half asleep. When we changed over to Lubovedski he became wide awake and very interested, and was sorry when it was finished.

I am ashamed to say I only remember two things about dinner. He produced from his pocket a wooden snake, painted with yellow and green spots, and very ingeniously made so that it squirms about when it is touched. He passed it round the table, saying how strange it is that even this can frighten some people, or give them a shock of dislike, because of heredity or upbringing, etc.

Then he began a very strange discussion with Mrs. P., saying it was not safe for her to walk in the streets of Paris. He asked if she knew what he meant and she said no: it then appeared that he was teasing her about the triple row of artificial pearls she was wearing. She said they were of no value and no one would strangle her for them, but he disagreed and said everybody knows that her husband, cousin, etc. would not let her appear in false pearls. This was not safe for her. So she said, all right; I'll throw them away. No, he answered, this would be foolish. She should keep them for black day - sometimes can be useful. She laughed and said, "Then I'll bury them". I did not understand all this: it obviously had some quite other meaning for her.

September 30th

We were only nine at lunch. Dwindling! In the morning I washed up with Rita and Mrs. P. and then Gurdjieff came in and sent us all off to the Turkish bath - we three went, and Lise, Rina and Katya. We went to St. Paul, or rather Rue des Rosiers, because Claridge's was closed and we found it cleaner and cheaper than St. Denis. I shall go there again.

At lunch when G. was looking for a director I stood back out of the way, and he told Mischa to be Director. I had thought he must be an experienced Director, and was glad that he had such a chance, but apparently this was not so. He didn't know the toasts or the way of arranging the table etc., and needed much prompting from Marthe. At Hopeless Idiots, if he had got through it quickly I should have been all right, but he muddled it and took a long time and so there was time for the emotion to build up inside me, and when I had to say the addition I could scarcely control my voice - scarcely speak even. G. looked at me quickly, as though in surprise, and then looked away again and made no comment.

We had a long discussion about the merits of the Hammam and how much he suffers from our emanations because we don't go to the Hammam, and how it is necessary to get rid of the residue of the second food, etc. And a lot about the "oily something" in the pores, and so on, and then, after a long talk, "But this enough philosophize - tell".

He teased Mischa about his English - "American English" - and told how Mischa and Nikolai went to America and made friends with the police, who gave a party for them when they left. (Mischa says he was 7 at the time, and Nikolai about 10).

Yesterday, lunch was soon over, so I went and spoke to Mr. G. in the reading room when the music was over. I knelt on the floor beside his chair, so that my face was more or less on a level with his, and I said something to the effect that I had worked for a year at the same exercise, and it was too difficult for me. But I needed something, badly, what was I to do?

He looked at me gravely, with great kindness, and then said, "If is too difficult, make easier. Do only half." He said, "You work too hard. Not forget your organism knows better. For instance –" and he repeated, emphasising, *'for instance* during menstruation, only do what wish. *Lie* more," and he made a pantomime of lying passively. He said, "Only do I AM". "Once every hour?" I said, and he replied that this already something, but can be more. I said, "At *least* once every hour", and he nodded. As I went out of the room he said again, "Not work so hard".

I was staggered by this, but I begin to understand.

So then about tonight. It was French night again, and also there were a few of our own people newly arrived. Katya went off again at 9. Rina read until Page arrived. Mr. G. had particularly told us to read the part in· 'Russia' about the Hammams. After that we started on 'Material Questions'. The reading was over about 11, and without thinking about it I went and joined the *chaine*. Suddenly from the crowd in the dining room I heard Mme. de S. call for "Elizabeth", and when I came to the door I realized that Lemaître had not come and I was to be Director. G. was waiting: I had 2 steps from the doorway to the table, to collect myself. Then I found O. in the Verseur's place, intent on pouring drinks, with her back to me. Suddenly I realized that she was furiously angry that I was to be Director. I know her in that mood and was prepared for trouble. Without speaking,

OCTOBER 1ST

I stood behind her waiting for her to make room for me to pass. I knew that it would be all I could do to get through the meal. It was the first large gathering of the French since their holidays and I could not spoil their evening for them. I knew that anything but passivity towards her would be my undoing. Then a curious thing happened. I saw her quite separately and apart from myself, a queer little vicious creature with beautiful hair on the top, quite away. Then Marcelle and José called to her and she moved, with a badly-done start of surprise, out of my way. So all through the meal I had this extraordinary situation to face: Mr. G. on my right, not making things very easy, but at the same time very accessible to me, and O. on my left, with quite distinct waves of unpleasantness coming out of her, and beyond her, very near her, Zlotti, who felt kind and consoling and friendly. I have never been much aware of people's atmospheres, but tonight I could feel distinctly the two entirely opposite states of those two women on my left. I should not have felt Zlotti more distinctly if she had held my hand. O., all through the meal, did everything possible to bitch me, and only during the second half did I begin to be able to take some conciliatory steps. I thought afterwards how strange it is actively to try to make things difficult for another person. My own likes and dislikes and negative criticisms always turn inwards and appear outwardly quite different from hers.

G. made me say the toasts in French and English, but I gave up the English after Arch Idiots and said them only in French. (There were one or two new French people there who did not speak one word of English). Afterwards G. played beautiful music, thin and small and very long; quite unlike any of the others. I sat alone in the dining room, in the dark, to hear it.

Later R. and I went to the Deauville with Doris and Olga, and we talked over the evening until about 2.30.

October 1st

Katya reappeared this morning ...
We went on with 'Material Questions' before lunch. G. enjoyed the reading (Rina read) and we went on till 3 o'clock.

Lunch was very entertaining. I was Director and there were about a dozen of us. Gurdjieff said that Barbara looked at him like cow, and said to Pierre that perhaps *he* could explain why? He then told the story of the cow with full details, and even said, "cow not cunning", which made me laugh. There followed a long discussion about Barbara's name, all sorts of wiseacring from various people about roots and what not.

In the evening we finished 'Material Questions', Entwhistle reading this time, so we did not start dinner till midnight.

Gurdjieff was full of the new "*château*" and arrangements for the party there tomorrow. He talked about practically nothing else. Mme. de S. wasn't there. O. was; not a bit malicious tonight, but not exactly amiable either!

Once again, though the evening was entertaining, the only really exciting bit was about Hopeless Idiots - "this small aim," etc.

October 2nd

I went early to the café, Gurdjieff was not there, but I met him on the way back at his garage. He greeted me across the road, so I went across and told him that I would like to go to London tomorrow for one day, and asked his approval. He said at once, "must-it be evening here", frowning a little, and I said, "Oh, yes; evening here, but I would like to go tomorrow morning". He agreed readily enough, nodding in a satisfied manner and said, "Even might be good". "Not for me". "No, but perhaps for me", and he gave me the message about John's mother. I said, turning to go, that I had been to the care to find him, and he said, "Come there now; coffee drink". So I went, gladly. I sat opposite to him: he drank tea and Perrier and distributed Hershey bars to various people. One tidy little girl of about ten or eleven came in, with her prayer book in her hand: she did not speak; he gave her a Hershey bar, she gave a little bob and said, "*Merci, Monsieur*" and went on her way. He said her mother used to bring her when she was a baby in her pram, and she had been every Sunday ever since.

We talked about Katya, and his *gaz*, and various things, but we were often silent. I was intensely happy. I was there more than an hour, and felt close to him. When Gabo arrived, with another Russian, I left after a few minutes. G. said it was very important to go tonight to the *Château*, "first times", because when I go again everything will be different: it will be "centre world Beelzebub".

I went to the Russian church with R.

Before lunch Rina read (very well) the beginning of 'Karpenko'. When we finished the incident of the firing range, Mr. G. told us to go to lunch, as he wanted to be early today. At the beginning of the meal he made a great show of being cross about everything. I had expected some such manifestation, after his amiability in the café this morning. It was his behaviour, rather than what he said, though he had one or two minor explosions with Lise and Marthe, but he let all this go as soon as he had finished preparing the *salade*, taking up his bottle of Calvados and saying, "Ah, Mr. Ahoon, how do you do?" and then turning to me with a smile, as though to say, end of round one. From then on all was roses, roses. We went through the meal quickly, and reached Zigzag Idiots. He gave me a *lot* of things to eat, and said I must be an example, such position have as Director.

Nearly all the conversation was about this evening's party at the *château*. Gabo and George were continually popping in and out, wanting instructions or telling of domestic disasters, etc. G. was anxious to sleep before his departure at 7, so we all left quickly after the meal, without waiting for music. (He had not, in any case, suggested coffee and music, as he almost always does).

The party of guests went off at various times and by various means. The two Entwhistles went at 5, by car, with their two babies, Rina and Emil Hana, the Elliots, Olga and Malcolm went by train at 5.30, Mr. G. himself left at 7 and Mme. Duprez at 7.15. I was left behind, Mrs. P. having taken my place, and was told to telephone to Lemaître and get him to bring me. He was very reluctant and didn't really know where the *château* was and didn't want to get back so late, etc., and would not be persuaded. So I had a peaceful early dinner and came back to the hotel to write this.

They took with them tonight to La Paroisse the "music" (both Gurdjieff's instrument and the Webster recorder) and 'Karpenko' to read, so it should be a good evening. I hope it is all going as he wants it: we do all want it to be a success. He was again rather 'cross' when he left this evening, but whether because he had just woken up or because he was regretting the whole undertaking, I don't know. He has looked tired yesterday and today.

2.30 a.m. I can't think why I imagined I should be able to sleep! I thought of all my stay here since I first arrived in my suicidal state, and how intense has been the feeling of Paradise and Hell, and what an irreplaceable experience it is, and what a tragedy to pass through life without knowing this.

At 12.15 Pierre telephoned from the *Château* to say that Mr. G. has been asking for me and blaming poor Mme. de S. for arranging badly (she of course did not know that G. had specially told me to be there, and she had told Page to take the last place, as Mr. G. might need him), and saying that he could easily have brought me himself, and that he had particularly wanted me to be there, etc. All the evening I have suffered because I knew I should have been there, and that Mr. G. had a reason for wanting me there, and I could not go. I was quite sure that he meant it when I spoke with him this morning in the street. When Mrs. P. was taking my place in the car she said, in any case I hadn't been invited, had I? And when I said, yes, most definitely I had been, she said with a knowing smile, "Oh, I shouldn't take too much notice of that if I were you", which would normally have filled me with foreboding, but this time I was not in the least shaken. I didn't say anything to her, because she is an Esteemed Person, but to me I said, "No, this time I know better". I sent Mr. G. a message by Pierre. Pierre said Mephisto is being Director, and rather floored by having to do the toasts in both languages, for the benefit of the "Notarius", who is there with his wife.

October 3rd

The party returned about 9.30. Rina had spent a couple of hours sitting in a chair by the fire, and the rest having spent those two hours in bed: there was only that time between the end of dinner and the departure of the train. Apparently the evening was a great success and Mr. G. was very pleased though very tired.

I left for London at about 3.15.

October 5th

As soon as I arrived in Paris I went to the café, Gurdjieff was not there, and I thought I was too late, but the proprietor told me that "*il vient de venir*," so I went back to the hotel, had some coffee, talked to Rina and returned to the café,

This time Mr. G. was there. He raised his hand to wave to me and called, "You here already?" and smiled. I really thought he was pleased to see me. I sat down at his table and he said, "Café, thé - take what wish", but I said, "No, thank you, I don't want anything: I only came to ask you one thing." He said, "Ask, ask", so I told him all the rigmarôle about my going or not going to America and how I must cancel my ticket today or never, so ... may I go or not? He looked past me, down the street, and I looked at him, at his strange, unmoved face, and wondered what he saw. After a silence, he said, "Ticket have already?" "Yes". "Then make this *promenade*." I thought I had misheard. I had to be sure. "I *can* go?" "Yes." He nodded gravely. "Can be good. Necessary many countries see." I couldn't help smiling at that, and he, after looking at me for a moment, smiled too. He knew what I was thinking. He went on, "Speak with Mme. de Salzmann. Very perhaps can orrange what we travel together. Will be good companions". As I got up to go he said, "Come lunch half past one", and gave me two sweets in case I should be hungry in the meantime. It is strange, but I have so accustomed myself to the idea that I would *not* go to America with him that now I can't believe that I will. It doesn't seem to be real in some way. In any case of course there are still many obstacles and difficulties in the way. I did not feel excited. I felt quite indifferent. I went back to the hotel and spoke to Mme. Barras about rooms for the week-end, met Rina and walked up the street with her to the Belfast, talking and thinking only about the complications of the week-end ahead, until she had to ask me the result of my meeting with Mr.G.

Lunch was fun. There were there only R. and me, the two Grünwalds, Vera, Marthe, Eve, a Russian girl whom I didn't know, and Tchechovitch. Mme. G. doesn't speak one word of English, so before lunch Marthe read (at high speed!) 'Religion' from the French version, and I did the toasts in French. Gurdjieff does not seem very well, and Rina says his leg is troubling him again, but he was in very good form at lunch and laughed and made us laugh. He ate half a sheep's head, but nothing else.

He made a recording afterwards, on the wire machine - the Webster machine has gone to London - and it played back very badly, with a wobble, so he told Lise to break off in the middle, and we went home.

At dinner we were even fewer. R. read beforehand from 'Skridlov' and at the end G. came in and was amused to see seven women in the room and no men. "Now not *interesse* me. Forty years, forty five *avant*, very much interested me. Not now". He turned to Vera and said something rather indistinctly to her in French which R. and I did not hear properly - something about how in such a place he had been very rich and had had four women.

At dinner he ate almost nothing. He said his *gaz* was bad and sent for his tablets. He did not even bother to eat *hors d'oeuvres,* and sent away the sheep's head that was brought to him, and gave almost the whole of his plate to Rina, who was *Egout.* The food was delicious, but there was so much of it: I was still choking down lumps of delicious steak when he had finished his melon. He drank the first four toasts in quick succession, but after that we went more slowly. Of the whole party there, R., Marthe and Emil Hana were Squirming Idiots, and everybody else was Square. G. was much amused by this. He talked about the pictures, and his proposed expedition on Saturday to the chdteau, and how now it is called "Hotel de la

Gare", but soon it will be known as "*Coin pour reposer Auteur Belzebuth*", His *gaz* was better after the tablets, but he didn't seem very well on the whole. He did not make a recording afterwards, but played two old "musics".

We came away about 1.30, and Rina, Emil and I went for a walk round the Arc de Triomphe.

October 6th

At both the meals yesterday, and today at lunch, I felt a most intense love for Mr. G., and because of this a freedom and release from all my usual burdens, real and imaginary, such as I have never known before. Today there was one moment when I was sitting looking at him while he cut up a cucumber or something, and I was thinking, "I *will* work, I *will* give him something in return", and I will even for this one momentary experience, if it stood by itself and nothing went before it, or came after; and as I looked at him he turned his head and looked at me with such a smile that I had to turn away after a moment - I *dared* not look at him any longer. As I turned away, so did he, back to his cucumber.

He ate very much more today. Baked potato with butter, which he always likes, and Rina was very crafty about the soup: she persuaded him to taste it, and he liked it so much that he sent out to the kitchen for a brown bowlful, and ate it all.

Tonight was French night. At 8.30, Rina and I were the only two English, so we sat in the passage and listened to the French reading. But by 10.30 the Kings, David Jones and Mr. Entwhistle had arrived. I sat in the piano corner and Rina ran in and out with plates. Lemaître was Director, and I watched him very carefully and tried to learn the French groups' idiots, and listened attentively to make sure that I do the French version properly. "*Toutes les femmes hysteriques*" - I always hear myself saying, "*tous les femmes ...*"

Mr. and Mrs. King took their usual places as Father and Mother, and when we reached Round Idiots - Mrs. K.'s idiot - G. pounced on Lemaître for calling her "Madame King". So Lemaître tried again with "Madame *Mère*", but this also was not approved; he was told to call her simply, "*Mère*". Then G. began to talk about this. How there are three "*mères*" at 6, Colonels Renard, first and second and third, according to age, and he went on to tell, in a wonderful mixture of French and English, what the "*très important archange*" asked God, and God's reply, etc. This was the main subject of the evening. He has often said this to the English - possibly because English children come more often to the flat - but one or two of the French to whom I spoke afterwards had not heard it before.

Mr. G. was not well tonight. His "*gaz*" was bothering him and he seemed very tired. He said he had had to speak "tete a tete" with not less than forty people today, and they had all caused him "*souci*". He improved a little as the time went on, though he ate practically nothing. The evening ended early, and at 12.45 the Kings, Rina, David and I went to the café on the corner of the Avenue Carnot.

After lunch today, Rina, Mrs. King and I drank coffee with Lise, Mme. Tracol and Anne-Marie, and Mrs. King told all that she had heard from her husband of Wednesday's meeting in London. I purposely avoided saying anything to Mr. G., as I expected him to have a first-hand account. He did ask Mr. King a little about it tonight.

October 7th

The Bennetts arrived with Kate at about 2, while we were reading.

Mr. B. was Director; I was *Verseur*. We were, once again, very few. Mr. G. is now on a diet which, Mr. B. says, he used to use for a week or two at a time at Fontainebleau - dry rusks soaked in a basin of milk, cream and yoghurt. One glass of alcohol. He was not at all well at lunch, and left while we had been only a few minutes at the table and had drunk only two toasts. He told Mr. B. to take his place, and went off with Gabo for massage and rest. When he had gone, Mr. B. told us all about the happenings at the meeting in London on Wednesday and Thursday nights. We had been longing to hear all about it.

Then we left, and an hour later went to the Gare du Nord

to meet Mme. de S. Marthe and Mischa were also there to meet her. The Adies and Elspeth Champcommunal were on the same train. When she had gone we went to a café and then hurried back for the movements. I tried to work, but I have rarely felt so clumsy.

In the evening we went on reading 'Pogossian' and broke off just at the amusing part about the fight in the café on the quay at Smyrna.

Several of the French group came to supper after the movements, so the room was quite full. I was in my corner and very happy. G. talked very much about the *château*, and made arrangements for lunch there tomorrow. He complained of *'gaz'* and ate the same food as he did at lunch.

October 8th

Several of us went off early to hire two large Renaults, each holding eight people, for the expedition to La Grande Paroisse. It was a lovely day, with bright sun. After various vicissitudes, we set off just after 11. Mephisto had gone ahead with his family; Lise, Marthe and José, and Mr. G. started about ten minutes before we did, with Mme. de S., Gabo and George. Mr. B. drove the first of our two cars, with Mrs. B., Kate, Dorothy and the two Adies, while David followed with Mr. and Mrs. King, Rita and Keith, Rina and me. We caught up Mr. G.'s car at some place on the way where he stopped for petrol, and followed him into the Forest of Fontainebleau, where we went by devious paths until it turned into a winding cart-track going steeply uphill. So we all stopped, turned after a lot of manoeuvering, and came back again. No one quite knew whether G. had meant to go that way or whether he was lost, but the beech trees were lovely in the sun and we all enjoyed ourselves. We passed the Prieuré and went on to the *château*. This was much nicer than I had expected: a little house built above the railway on a steep slope of poor soil, with a view over the river. There is a patch of neglected kitchen garden, some good out-houses and a few scrubby fruit trees. Tall chestnut trees along the hedge by the road, a well and a few flowers, marigolds, unpruned rose bushes and what not. The house has a large room on the left where we lunched, a bar on the right and a good kitchen, easy to work in and keep clean, etc. Upstairs are four or five bedrooms. (The Entwhistles have moved in there to live, ·as he has to be there so much.) The attics, or rather one large attic, is accessible at present only by a ladder (G.'s "*escalier* make chic up-house"), but this is where the outside double staircase comes in, with a terrace to be made on the slope behind the house, and the mosaic with the Enneagram, etc.

Mr. G. was wearing his great-coat with the astrakhan collar and his red fez. When he arrived, while we were exploring, having drinks, etc., he sat in the dining room with his feet on another chair, and rested a little. A small fire had been lit, and there were flowers on the tables, arranged - the tables, I mean - in a T-shape. The walls are pale green and there are large windows on two sides. It looked nice. Lise, Marthe, José and Mme. Tracol were already hard at work in the kitchen: Rina and I looked in to offer help, but it was all going so smoothly and efficiently and *quietly* that we came away.

At lunch Rina and I were at the far end of the table, but we heard G. talk about Hopeless Idiots, and later Mr. B. told us that he had also talked about *obyvatels*[1] - I would have liked to have heard that. I gather that he talked about the Notarius (who was there) in connection with this, and said in effect that this was why he could feel at home with us, because he has these qualities of an obyvatel.

We left at once when lunch was over, and had a break-down on the way home, causing Mme. de S. to miss her small group. But at least she was back in time to take the movements, and Mr. B. says she gave a marvellous talk on taking the movements seriously, and on how to do the turning - as though you are walking along the street.

At dinner, Gurdjieff was obviously very tired indeed, and certainly one would have said that he should not have driven the car today. He persists with his diet, under the surprisingly stern eye of Dr. Egg. He talked about how Lise is not a

---

1   Roughly, a good, honest householder. See P. D. Ouspensky, In Search of the Miraculous, Routledge & Kegan Paul, 1950, p. 362.

musician; she is "Doctor of Vibrations" - the only one, unique. Mr. B. said surely also Hadji-Asvatz Troov? Mr. G. said, yes, of course. And then that the Hadji had been very ill and they had all been concerned about him, but now he is all right again, and working on "one problem - why God make louse and tiger?" But I am afraid I can't remember the rest of the conversation.

G. wore his new brown tweed suit, and when he said he had forgotten where it was made, Mme. de S. said, "So-and-so made it for you before you went to America last time". He frowned, and said, "*Là-bas* they see already?" but she reassured him! We went afterwards to the café.

October 9th

We heard that Mr. G. is to stay in bed today, and will not come in for lunch, but we are to come as usual. He is really taking his illness seriously, I am glad to see. Evidently he wants to go to America.

So we went over, and started reading, but at 2.15 he came in as usual, wearing a dressing gown, and saying as usual, "Director! I think enough. Already vibrations your voice mixed with vibrations your tape-worm. Come, eat; occupy-it place."

He was very tired and cut the meal short: we had very few toasts. At the end, coffee was served at the table, while Lise played music in the next room. He looked at us all while the music was being played, with a little smile on his face, smoking and drinking his coffee. We left immediately afterwards. As we went out of the room, Mr. B. said, perhaps we oughtn't to come tonight? "Why?" "Isn't it better for you to rest?" He said, "No, no; come half past ten", and added that he can't lie all day, like an idiot! I thought of Mrs. E., with her blue eyes open very wide, saying earnestly that an effort continuously sustained is much more difficult than one intense short effort, and how wonderful it is that Mr. G. never, never misses a meal, year in and year out - "I think that's *wonderful*" she said, "much more wonderful than killing yaks. Though that must be very wonderful, too ... "

Before dinner Mr. B. read not at all well, for some reason. He made mistakes and did not seem to be paying the least attention. He does that occasionally. Perhaps he is over-tired.

At dinner G. had a long conversation with Mr. Bloemsma about organizing a group in the Hague. Bloemsma asked if it would be a good idea to introduce a custom of dining together after a meeting, occasionally, saying that this could be organized at his house. Mr. G. said that this sort of thing can be good, but they must not have always the same host; they must take turns in this. But much was in Russian, so I lost it.

October 10th

The Bennetts left in the morning from Le Bourget. Rina and I went to see them off, and I was very acutely aware of the end of something. I remembered how Mr. B. went away after that first week-end in March, when he brought me here, and how I felt when I was left alone, and I thought how differently I feel now. This week seems somehow to be full of 'last times', but without regrets. Regrets about myself, of course, but no feeling of 'nevermore'.

It was said that Mr. G. was not coming to lunch. Mme. de S. was not there either. Adie was Director - a difficult job in those circumstances, and he did not manage it well. Marthe was the only person not from London. Rosemary Nott, just arrived, was Egout, and Rina and I sat facing her, at the foot of the table. A combination of concern about Mr. G., English stodginess and Adie's sonorous delivery of the toasts, as of one making some dreadful pronouncement of future retribution not long to be delayed, produced a morgue-like atmosphere which Rina and I tried hard to combat. We started discussions about this and that at our end of the table, helped by N. and Dr. M., but Mr. Adie obviously disapproved of this and glared witheringly at us whenever he said, "Attention, *please!*", making us feel like naughty members of the Lower Fifth. So I called down the table to Rosemary, asking her to tell us the latest news of the movements in London; how are they being organized, etc.? She responded, as one would expect, with enthusiasm, and the atmosphere lightened considerably. Then, in a silence, someone said they hoped the new arrangements would put an end to any remnants of internecine strife, and Rina said, oh, surely yes, now all that sort of thing would be forgotten. (She managed the whole of this incident extremely well. Only In one small point could I see any indication of how bitterly she had felt it, and even perhaps still feels it, and that one point I am sure was lost on the men: only the women would have noticed it.) She went on to tell, briefly and very amusingly, the incident at the Belfast Hotel last year, when she was not allowed to join the members of another group for coffee, after lunch at Mr. G.'s flat, saying that *that* sort of thing would never happen again. I was much surprised at the vehemence with which both A. and N. repudiated this: they were both obviously extremely agitated by it, and instead of replying in Rina's own spirit, denied it with most damning protests. But she laughed at them, and stuck to her point.

And then we heard Mr. G. coming along the passage, and he came in and took his place at the table. He was wearing a dressing gown and looked much better. He teased A. about his English, and, though we were far past Hopeless Idiots, made me give the addition, so that he could speak about the necessity of having an aim. We went as far as Born Idiots. Then coffee and music in the dining room, and so home.

There was to be a French reading at 8.30, but Lise and Marthe asked us, the English, please not to come till 10.30 unless we understood French, as they did not want to arrange an English reading in Lise's room - one can hear through the wall of those two rooms, and it would have disturbed Mr. G.

D.B.J. gave us some money today, so Rina and I, with nothing to do at the flat, went to the Opera. I had never been inside it before and was glad to see it at last. We heard the first two acts of 'Tristan'. At least, even that is not quite true: we left at 10 o'clock, after the duet in the second act, but we were both quite happy to miss all the struggling about at the end of the act. It was an unusual experience for both of us. Rina said it was the first time literally for years that she had enjoyed such a thing for itself, by herself, and for the first time she felt free of that particular bondage. I, who have my own reasons for loving Tristan, felt an acute enjoyment of the music, but remained free. Those two and a half hours were very good for us; we came away feeling much refreshed. I know that if I hear something like that I can be collected, but that if I see slapstick comedy, for example, I simply become a custard pie or whatever it is. Both states are caused by external influences, not by my 'doing'. It is merely a case of one influence waking me up and the other lulling me to sleep.

There were about 60 people at the flat, a huge crowd. G. seemed better, and sent for his little hand organ at the end of the meal and made a recording while he sat at the table - his first recording for several days. But he was not satisfied with it, and did not let Lise finish playing it back. He said, "Head is here, hands here, but not heart". And then with a wide smile, "Tomorrow will be heart also".

October 11th

Mr. G. insisted on getting up and going out this morning for a business appointment, with the result that at lunch he looked quite frighteningly tired. And we *were* so awful! All English. Me in my corner, Rina dodging about, Adie intoning the toasts. R. and I thought just about everything was done that shouldn't have been - even to the Director offering Mr. G. unsuitable foods. Yesterday, when Mr. G. came in late, he asked A. if he had made me give the addition, and said he should have - "this your fault", etc. So today, after the toast to Hopeless Idiots, A. called on me for the addition. I did not like this, and did not want to say it unless Mr. G. asked for it, because he doesn't ask for no reason, and was too tired to talk today. I looked from him to the Director and back again. He watched me, but gave no sign. A. asked again, insistently, so, still looking at Mr. G., I got up slowly and began, "By the way ... " He stopped me at once, saying quietly that this was not always necessary; not today, for instance, there were no new people. So I sat down again. The chief thing I remember about lunch is that G. *yawned* during the reading: the first time I have ever seen him do it!

In the evening there were movements. Many people arrived from London: there were as many in the audience as there were working. Mme. de S. came in rather late. Mr. G. of course was not expected and the class went on as usual. But at 7.45 the door opened and G. came in. He was wearing his ordinary dark European clothes, with a very furry Homburg hat, which partly accounted for his appearance, but I did think he looked *dreadfully* ill. Very dark round his eyes, and his face quite sunken, and moving very slowly. I felt a sort of shocked clutch at my inside when I saw him. He sat down with his feet on another chair - Lise lifted them for him - and we at once did No. 17, the Multiplication, which he likes so much. He left after more than an hour, and Lise and Marthe with him, but before he went he gave us the beginning of a truly amazing new movement - No. 39. One sits cross-legged on the floor, and Solange came out and counted aloud, sitting at the side, "Un, deux, trois ... " and so on. When we had worked at it for a while, G. stopped us and made "*un petit addition*". Then he said we could practise this "in *maison*", and next time he would add to it. (But next time I shan't be here.)

There were many people at dinner, and I was in and out all the time.

He looked better, but was very tired. He said little. Lemaître was Director, and A. - Verseur - repeated the toasts in English. When Hopeless Idiots came, Lemaître and Adie both called for me, but I refused to be drawn. I laughed at them a little bit, and shook my head and went out again. Then Mr. G. called for me, and I came back and gave the addition.

We went away quickly.

October 12th

Healey read at lunch and Nicholls in the evening. Hoare Director. I have very little to say about the day. G. said almost nothing, not even correcting Mr. Hoare for mistakes in the toasts. He did not ask for the addition. I have been wondering about this still existing restraint between the groups and how opposed this is to working for G., and how we *must* overcome it. All the women in all the other groups are very kind and friendly (with one, or possibly two, exceptions), but *all* of them are as nice as possible and so easy to get on with. I believe the difficulty is caused by the men. I must think about this.

October 13th

I don't know if G. was making a great effort at lunch, or if he is really a little better. At 9 I went over to wash up, with Mrs. Juer, B.C.M. and Denis C. We stood outside for 20 minutes, not daring to ring for fear of disturbing G., and were rewarded: later Lise came and thanked us and said he had slept all through our arrival.

October 14th

I had to break off then, and now it is Friday morning and we have been airborne about 5 minutes. In a York. There was a fog, and we spent one hour at Le Bourget. B.E.A. and B.O.A.C. aircraft didn't take off and we were told there would be an indefinite delay, but Air France provided a path finder. Now we are above the fog, in hot bright sun, with our shadow moving after us over the fog below. But about yesterday.

Mr. G. said little at lunch, but as we were going, H. asked if we could come in the evening and G. said yes, half past ten, but not go away like last night. Last night he came back and found everybody gone. (Mme. de S. chivvied us away after dinner, before the music, and we heard afterwards that he was angry about this.) This behaviour, he said, was artificial. When one came here to a meal, it was necessary to complete it, otherwise it all became artificial. One could eat elsewhere, but everywhere else is artificial, and does you no good. In England at the moment it is not artificial, but here (in France) it is. Be careful not to let this poison grow also in England. This was all addressed to H. and Dr. W., (though the latter did not appear to be listening and could give no account of it afterwards) and what I have written here is what I heard, as I stood beside Dr. W. But when later I asked H. what had been said, to make sure I had got it right, he said casually, "Oh, I shouldn't worry too much about that - he was talking about food". And Mrs. H. chimed in, with her lovely gentle little voice and her velvety smile and said, "He was saying the food everywhere in France is poison, except at the flat: in London there ·is less food, but it is not poison." So there we are: two interpretations. Or one, or six ...

At dinner (French night) Mme. de S. was there and G. made a few mild little jokes and actually roared at Marthe about something or other, so he must have been feeling better. Until tonight I had not told him that I wanted to go to England, hoping that an opportunity would arise without my having to make one, but it didn't, so as everyone was leaving the dining room I sat down in *Egout's* place and said I must leave in the morning to make arrangements so that I could join him in America. He said, "But I not will go", shaking his head and with a disapproving wave towards his tummy. "You won't go?" "No, not will go, such state have." I made approving and sympathetic noises and he went on, "In 20 days, then I go. Perhaps you also can arrange?" I said yes, and was about to say goodbye to him but H. approached him from the other side and he turned away. I went, not wanting to tire him further.

We had afterwards two recorded 'musics', then he played one, and then that was played back, so we had four in all, and were later than we have been for many days. I had the most charming and affectionate farewell from Lise. Rina got up and came with me to the Gare des Invalides (a real effort for her!), but B.C.M. overslept and we didn't disturb him. R. gave me a spray of carnations and mimosa and a book for the journey. I was prepared for a long wait at le Bourget. While I was writing, we crossed the English coast. I looked down and there was the beach, and a long wave breaking sideways, and the sea, no colour at all. I shall have plenty of time.

October 16th

ENGLAND The news from Paris is not encouraging. Mr. G. went to the café on Friday morning and afterwards drove himself to the bath, but at the movements in the evening he quite collapsed. Now he must be for a fortnight in bed, and they want him to stop smoking, and some sort of drug is being sent to him from America. In the circumstances I thought I had better ask permission to return to Paris, so at 5 o'clock I telephoned to Mme. de S. and asked her if I might come back on Friday. She sounded really quite pleased, and said she thought it might be a good thing, but she must ask Mr. Gurdjieff and will tell R.H. the answer. She said would I tell Mr. B. that he can come this week end, but not to bring anyone with him. For me it was different, but a new visitor must not come. At the same time say nothing of this to Mr. G., as he will be angry if he thinks people are being prevented on his account. When I rang off, she said, "Goodbye, dear" - strange that even her voice can transmit her marvellous being.

October 21st

This has been a very frightening day.

Mr. B. and I took a taxi when we arrived in Paris, telling the driver to go past Mr. Gurdjieff's café, just in case, but he wasn't there. However, as we passed the café we saw one of the Russians on the pavement, so Mr. B. stopped the car, got out and went back to him, to ask for news.

I stood on the pavement by the car, looking up the street quite aimlessly, when suddenly I saw Mr. G. coming, with Bernard beside him. They were just level with the garage, coming towards the café. I had a sudden detailed sight of them, perfectly clear in every detail, a shock all through me, as though I had seen a miracle, but in a moment I was running down the street to fetch Mr. B. We came back together, and by then Mr. G. was at the fruit shop, poking at things with his stick. As we came up, he was saying, "special for English ... "

He was wearing his coat with the Astrakhan collar, sheepskin boots, a brown and red woolen scarf folded over his chest, and his black Astrakhan cap. His appearance gave me a shock. He looked so ill, his face very dark, with black rings sunken under his eyes.

This is the first time I have looked at him and seen an old man.

I was looking quite unfamiliar, with a hat and so on, but he turned and recognized me at once, with a smile, and then looked at Mr. B. and was obviously very glad to see him, smiling with his eyes sparkling almost in their normal way. (He has trimmed his mous*tâche* very neatly; it is noticeably smaller).

He stayed at the shop to buy bananas and grapes and then went on down the street, walking *very* slowly, with Mr. B. and Bernard. He said it was the first time he had been out, and I saw that he was treating himself very carefully, which is not at all usual with him. When they went on to the care I returned to the hotel, sorted out the luggage, greeted Mme. Barras and went up to talk to Rina.

When Mr. B. and Bernard returned, they said that Mr. Gurdjieff was "experimenting" with himself, drinking more, going out, etc., to see the result. I don't like it.

At lunch I liked it less. We went on reading till 3 before G. came in. He wore a dressing gown and his fez, and José lifted his feet on to the cushion for him. He looked round at us all for a minute or two, and then began to doze. I have heard from several people that he sleeps very much of the time now.

At 3.30 we went in to lunch. It is extraordinary and frightening to see the extent to which he is separated from his body and its surroundings. He scarcely spoke, and when Mr. B. spoke to him he brought himself back in order to give a brief answer. Several times when I looked up I saw him looking at me as though he ought to know who I am but couldn't place me. I expect if I had been in my corner he would have known me, but sitting at the table where I so rarely am I am sure he didn't recognize me.

Mr. B. kept the meal going exactly as usual, but I don't know where Mr. Gurdjieff was. Afterwards Lise played two 'musics', G. going into the sitting room to listen, and then we went away very quickly. The music was most wonderful.

But I was alarmed by what I saw.

Neither Mme. de S. nor Mr. G. came to the movements, not Lise nor Marthe. Solange took the class, and when music was wanted Mme. Blondeau provided it. We worked hard and afterward I was very tired. Mrs. B. arrived at about 6.30.

One or two French people came to dinner; Marie-Claude, José and Philippe. Mr. G. talked much more and made a few jokes, but I thought his state more alarming than at lunch. He is so desperately tired. (I forgot to say that at lunch he did seem to have some contact with Mme. de S., but he seemed entirely unaware of anyone else). I noticed very much his - submission, I think is the word - to the arrangements of Marthe and Lise: he looked at Marthe as though she were in charge, and made no comment or objection or reaction of any kind. He was pleased with the "salt" that the Bennetts had brought to him from England, and said, "Bravo, English", and said to Mr. B., "Remind me when you go and I will send corresponding present for the English." But he did seem awfully feeble.

After two beautiful musics, recordings of course, we left, and the Bennetts, Emil, Mrs. P., Tilley and I went to the Arab care. We returned to our hotels at about 1.30.

October 22nd

Rina left last night.

Mrs. P., Tilley and I went to do the washing up this morning, and when we left just after ten, Mr. Gurdjieff was up and about in his dressing gown. I had only a distant view of him and could not see how he looked. I went back to the Rena. Later I went out shopping with the Bennetts, and on the way home we went down the Rue des Acacias to buy slippers for Mrs. B. Mr. B. was ahead of us, and suddenly I saw him begin to hurry, and when we came round the corner he had disappeared. I said to myself, "He is in the care with Mr. Gurdjieff," and was seized with a feeling of great unease. As we passed, we saw them sitting there, but when we returned five minutes later they were gone. I have heard, in bits here and there, what happened, but I don't know how accurate it is.

Apparently after his expedition yesterday he told Lise not on any account to let him go out, but this morning he forgot his appointment with the doctor and in fact all his instructions to Lise, and appeared, ready to go out as usual. It appears that

Page was with him, went with him to the care and there left him. He disregarded all Lise's attempts to stop him and she was afraid to tire him with arguments and irritation. So there he was at the care, quite unfit to be out and unable to get home. By chance no one was there of his usual people. Mr. B. said he was looking at the car on the far side of the road, but was unable to reach it, and of course he can't get into it without help. So Mr. B. helped him to the car and drove home with him. Mr. B. says he was terrified of an accident, as he was quite unable to drive and should certainly not be allowed to. (But who can stop him?)

He did not appear at lunch. About a dozen of us sat down without him, and we left at about 3.

He seems to have become so far separated from his body that he no longer cares - possibly no longer knows - what is happening to it. It was simply an habitual automatism that brought him to and from the café this morning. One good thing is that Mme. de S. is going to move into the flat straight away and stay with him.

Later The plan of Mme. de S. staying at the flat is changed. Instead she is going to try to persuade him to go to a clinic, where he will really have to submit to the treatment and where he will be safe from such goings-on as this morning's promenade. I hope he will agree to it.

Mme. de S. came to the movements at 8. Solange took the class. We were about 15 or so. Mrs. B. watched; Mr. B. and Bernard were working.

Mr. B. went to the flat just before 10.30, and found that we had better stay away. So we had dinner upstairs in Mrs. B.'s room. Tilley joined us, and we drank brandy and talked till after midnight.

It was most difficult to stay away from the flat tonight. My thoughts were there all the time, and I am sure it was the same for the others. It was particularly difficult as we were not told definitely to go or stay; we had to decide for ourselves.

About midnight Mr. B. went out and by chance met Mme. de S. coming away from the flat. She said we did right to stay away, and that G. is not well, though he had come in for a short time for dinner.

October 23rd

I went to breakfast at the Chevreuse and spent the whole morning there, first checking manuscripts with Mrs. B. and afterwards correcting while she worked with Tilley.

Mme. de S. came round at 12.30 to speak to Mr. B. It turns out that Mr. G. has at last found a corresponding doctor whom he trusts. A nurse is to come today, and if she cannot manage he will go to a clinic. We all felt greatly relieved that the whole thing seems to some extent to be getting organized. He is apparently better, though his heart is in a bad way.

We were told not to go to lunch - he is in bed, and must see no one today - so we four went with Tilley to the Petit Colombier.

I returned to the Rena to finish working on 'Material Questions'.

Emil came in to talk to me, but he had no later news. At 5.30 I went back to tea with the Bennetts: B.C.M. was there, Tilley, Kyril Kupernik and an American called, I think, Lutz. I wanted to be away.

Just before 7, Mme. de S. telephoned to tell Mr. B. that he could go round to the apartment - a wonderful happening, as we were told Mr. G. could see no one today, and Mr. B. leaves tomorrow. She said he is better.

Later Mr. B. returned sometime after 8 and said he had found Mr. G. better.

We, with Tilley, went to the Petit Colombier for dinner. We had a private room to ourselves, which was as well because we laughed a lot and talked about Mr. G. It was a pleasant hour: we were all so relieved that Mr. G. is better. We were told that he had wanted brains to eat, but on being told that there were none he asked instead for a baked potato. But there were brains on the menu at the restaurant, so Mr. B. got some uncooked from the kitchen and Tilley took them round to the flat. As we were sitting over our coffee, Mrs. Pearce came in, and Page and

Emil, so we were quite a large party. I was glad they came: it seemed a good thing.

Mme. de S., Lise, Gabo and all his nearests are doing everything possible. I have a feeling of 'us' against 'something', as though we are all holding a fort. None of us slept well. Not really surprising.

October 24th

It had begun to rain during the night. It is now 9.45 p.m. and the rain has not stopped or even diminished all day. It is cold, too; the central heating has been started up in the hotel. I went to breakfast at the Chevreuse with the Bennetts, and spent the morning with them, driving out with them to Le Bourget at 12.

During the morning, Mrs. P. came in with the most alarming reports from No. 6, which sent Mr. B. there at once, but thank goodness she had exaggerated, and he came back to report that Mr. G. had passed a very bad night but that his heart is a little better now. But really the position is much the same.

I watched the Bennetts go out to the aircraft in a bus, and saw them go into the plane. I would have stayed, but the petrol bowser was still there and obviously they would not be leaving yet. I thought it foolish to wait longer, so I went back to Paris through the rain.

I stayed in my room, cold and dark and damp, and listened to the rain and wrote various things and did some washing, and later Tilley came and we went out to dinner together. Afterwards I went with him to the Gare du Nord; he is leaving for England tonight. Then, wet through, back to No. 6 to ask for news before going back to bed.

There is no news, really. I saw Emil, who gave me coffee to warm me, and Lise, and while I was there in the kitchen Page and the Old Doctor came through. Mr. G. was asleep when I arrived, but he woke a few minutes later and I heard him shouting for Lise and talking to Dr. Hambaschidze - his voice is all right, anyway!

Apparently he slept a lot today and if anything, is a little better tonight. That is, his heart is said to be a little better, but I gather there is really no change one way or the other. Apparently he can't eat, or at any rate doesn't want to. He has milk and yoghourt and not much even of that. Lise prepared some lemon juice for him while I was there. So I came back here to write this and go to bed. I feel very much alone, although the little grey cat is asleep on my bed. Now I will sleep, and ask for news again in the morning. It is raining still.

October 25th

Mr. B. telephoned at 11.45 last night. I hadn't much news for him.

4.30 p.m. The news is definitely better. I went to the apartment and found everyone: Dr. Abadie, Mme.de S., Lise, Gabo, Mrs.P. and Emil. Apparently G. wanted company yesterday evening, and when Liliane and her husband arrived about 11.30 he had a table brought into his bedroom and they had dinner there, with Mrs. Pearce, Gabo and Dr. Hambaschidze. With toasts in Armagnac, etc. They went through the meal as quickly as possible so as not to tire him too much, but when Liliane and her husband had gone, just after 12, he called back Page and Mrs. P. and they had coffee and music! All this did him good, though Mrs. P. said he was obviously suffering by the end of the music, as he always does, it appears, after eating. But he had a good night and did not once call Lise. They have been giving him injections for his heart, which is now better, and, on his instructions, Mme. de S. today telephoned to Dr. Welch in New York, as Mr. Gurdjieff says he will take the treatment for the liver if Dr. W. comes over to give him the injections. (Apparently he likes this treatment, because it is something quite new that he doesn't know about.) They hope that by the time Dr. Welch arrives at the end of the week his heart will be strong enough for him to be able to have the liver injections. Georges was preparing a sheep's head for him in the kitchen this morning. Altogether everyone is much happier about him, and Mme. de S. says that the illness is really beginning to give way a little now.

I made two visits to the *pharmacie*, and afterwards went to the Rue du Bac to leave the typing for Mme. de S. Then with Mrs. P. to the Post Office to pay the telephone and gas bills at the flat, and then she and I went out to lunch together. The rain has stopped and it is a hot sunny day with a clear blue sky, so *everything* is right, even the weather. We had an amiable lunch and then went all the way to the Faubourg St. Denis for a Turkish bath, but found it closed! So we came back again, both quite overcome with relief, the sudden change in the weather, etc., and resolved to sleep until it is time for the movements.

I was relieved to hear that last night Mr. G. asked many questions about the goings-on in England, and obviously knew exactly what it was all about. He seems to have 'come back' again, which is to me much more encouraging and a better guide to the situation than all the variations in the state of his physical body.

Mme. de S. came to the movements, which is a good sign. Mme. Blondeau played, and Mme. de S. left before 8, having a rendezvous with the doctor. Dr. and Mme. Egg arrived during the movements. We worked, while Mme. de S. was there, on the new No. 39, and she spoke to us about the inner work. We practised several with Solange that we haven't done for a long time, with one or two that I haven't seen before. We left at 8.45.

I went to the little café in the Rue des Acacias and had some dinner, and went to the flat at about 10.45.

Emil and Lise were in the kitchen. She looked pale, but smiling and happy: she took both my hands, and when I asked if there is any news, she shook her head, smiling more than ever. Apparently Mr. G. had slept a lot today, and is sitting in what she calls an "Harm chair", dozing again. He ate a little fish for lunch, and she was preparing little pieces of boiled chicken for the evening. At about 5 he was suffering from "*gaz*" and had a rather bad fit of coughing, but nothing extraordinary. His blood pressure is noticeably improved.

Page was already in the flat, dozing in the dining room,

and the Old Doctor arrived while I was there. Lise said Mme. de S. had told her there are to be no more dinner parties in his room just yet, but the Old Doctor can have supper with him tonight. Mme. de S. arrived about 11, and Mrs. P. appeared just as I was leaving. Mme. de S. was firm in her intention of not dining there tonight: she says she only came to see him, and will not stay long. Really it is true, as Lise says, there is no news. He has not gone back at all since this morning, but has rather improved. His heart is certainly better. One can feel the atmosphere of lightheartedness as soon as one enters the flat.

Mr. B. telephoned at 11.45, and I also spoke briefly to Mrs. B. and C.M. For myself, I will make a new programme of work before I sleep tonight, and start the moment I wake. These everlasting good resolutions!

October 26th

The wind rose during the night and blew so hard that when I was half asleep I thought I was back again in Suffolk, listening to a rough sea. But the wind drowned all the early morning street noises, and I slept until Giselle brought my breakfast at 9! I reached the Rue de l' Assomption at 10, and had a lovely female session with Mme. Farman. As usual, I did not know how to choose, and longed to say, one of each, please! By 11 o'clock I was back again at No. 6. There the news is less good. It appears that G. did not sleep *at all* during the night, and Lise was up with him the whole time. Apparently at about 11.30 last night he asked the Old Doctor and Mrs. P. to dine in his room, and she told me she thought he looked quite ill again, even then. I stayed only about ten minutes; it seemed to me that there were enough people there, and Mr. G. and Lise were trying to get some sleep. At the door on my way out I met Mme. de S., due to meet Dr. Abadie there. I helped her out of the taxi and said I would not come back till the evening, but would she send a message to the hotel if anything was needed. As I turned to go, she spoke again, and I had a curious feeling that she wasn't speaking to me, but thinking aloud; simply a worried woman wanting to talk to someone. She said, "If we could find someone who knows about food, some doctor. I am sure that is what upset him." Then she turned away, and went into the house. Dr. Welch is due to arrive at 6.30 this evening. I went to the telephone exchange in the Boulevard de Vaugirard to look into and pay the No. 6 telephone bill for the last four months. Today the wind was so strong that it blew down the exhibition stand of metal girders by the Pont de l'Alma. The whole thing blew straight into the river, taking two trees with it.

Later Mr. G. has gone to the American Hospital. I am relieved, really. There was too much going on at the flat. His departure was typical. The ambulance men brought the stretcher to his room, but he wouldn't have this, and walked out into the hall and got on to the stretcher there, sitting back, saying, "Oy!" as he always does. He did not dress, but wore pyjamas, and his red fez on his head. He sat upright on the stretcher, and was carried away like a royal prince! All the family was clustered at the street door (the crusty old *concierge* was in tears!) and as they carried him across the pavement he made a little gesture, a sort of wave, with his hand and said, "*Au revoir, tout le monde!*" The last sight of him was as he was carried into the ambulance, sitting very upright, with his head up, his fez at a rakish angle and his cigarette between his lips. Somehow I could not tell how he looked, and I asked Emil, "Is he much changed?" But Emil, who also had not seen him for some days, said wonderingly, "I don't know". I know that feeling!

Mme. de S. and Dr. Welch went with him. Dr. W., who hasn't even seen his hotel yet, but went straight to Gurdjieff from the plane, is going to spend the night at the Hospital. Later they sent for Lise, who went off to see him about 11.30. I feel very restless. It is almost 2 o'clock, and I *will* sleep. I shall be at the hotel all day tomorrow, but I will contrive somehow to get news. Emil will pass on to me anything he hears.

October 27th

I did sleep, till 6. Mrs. P. has just been in - God bless her - to tell me the news. After the treatment last night he is very tired but immeasurably relieved. Apparently he sits there smiling and saying, "*Ah, bon!*" Dr. Egg and Dr. Welch are taking turns to be there all the time. They are less worried about his heart and his liver than they are about his lungs. Dr. Egg says they are in a bad state. Well, of course; they must have been bad for years. There is, of course, everything still to be done, but at least he is free of that intolerable discomfort. Mme. de S. and Lise are taking turns at being there all the time. It appears that he is perfectly happy in the Hospital, and likes it. He has a proper adjustable bed, which must make a great difference to his comfort.

Emil gave me an amusing account of Lise's packing. The suitcase which Gurdjieff took with him contained countless bon-bons for the nurses, and a tea spoon, in case the Hospital didn't have one!

Emil came again after lunch, but had no further news. He had left the flat because he was the only person there not Russian, and they were all glooming away in a truly Russian state - Sofya Ivanovna[1] in tears and Gabo, just returned from the Hospital, repeating again and again how "*fatigué*" he is. I believe they all thought that once the treatment was done G. would come straight home, cured. Though he is very seriously ill, they are also disappointed because there has been no miraculous recovery.

The little cat has been all day on my bed, purring like a dynamo.

1.45 a.m. Emil has just gone. We are all very worried. Mme. de S. says he is a *little* better this evening, better, that is, than he was this morning. They have been making all sorts of tests today, and specimens of this and that for analysis, which, though illuminating for the doctors, is terribly wearing for the patient. His heart is still all right. They are trying to build up his strength. Dr. Welch says he is "vastly sick". Mme. de -S. says she is not going into the room while the doctor is there, as the effort of recognizing two people is too great. Even Lise has no place there at the moment, poor dear; he recognizes her only with difficulty. But Mme. de S. does say he is a little better.

I went out about 8 to supper with Emil, to the little restaurant <u>in the Grande Armée</u>. He hadn't been there before, and liked

[1] Gurdjieff's sister.

the sawdust on the floor and the brass rails and the aspidistra.

I am very tired. So is everyone else I have seen today. We all have this same feeling of responsibility transferred from us, now that G. is in the Hospital.

Emil told me all about diving for pearls off the coast of Arabia.

October 28th

I woke full of the most ridiculous forebodings. I don't know what it is that I am afraid of - unless it is just that, not knowing - because I really do not believe that he will die. In spite of his age and the certainty that he is very seriously ill. Also it is bitterly cold and I haven't got enough warm clothes. I don't care about those things for themselves, but they probably help to push me, spineless and helpless as I am, towards gloom and despondency. I took a resolve, though, that no one else should see this, and began by teasing Giselle when she came with my coffee.

At ten Mrs. P. telephoned, wanting me to do various things for her.

She told me that Mr. G. has had a fairly good night, the glucose is doing him good, and they are going to try giving him a little food today. So things are a little better, even if it is only local ups and downs again.

6.30 At 11 I had a message to go to F.'s place, which I did. It took a long time, but it was highly entertaining. After lunch, alone, I went up to the Belfast to fetch Mrs. P.'s things, and from then on until this moment she and I cleaned the dining room at the flat. It was a true Augean stable, and we haven't finished yet: there is still the floor to be scrubbed tomorrow. All day we have had no news from the Hospital. At last Lise came in; she had been out since 8.30 a.m. Mme. de S. chased her away from the Hospital at mid-day to lunch with her family, so she had no very immediate news. She told us that all the time she was there he had been "*très agité*", but that really there is no change. Then she returned to him.

Mme. Duprez looked in soon after to say that his condition

is "stationary". Mrs. P. telephoned to Marthe, who said that he is dozing very much. Altogether, little change.

After the movements I came back with Emil to No. 6 and had some supper with him, while poor Sofya Ivanovna wandered about looking worn out, but unable to eat or rest. It was very quiet and peaceful in the flat. We sat as long as we wanted over our coffee, and then there was a knock at the door and Mrs. P. came in with Mischa. I must say that when I saw Mischa's face I felt perfectly sick and giddy with fear.

He went straight to Sofya Ivanovna and spoke to her in Russian. He was telling her to go with him to the Hospital. Mrs. Pearce, having asked for some supper, went to take off her things. When Mischa was free, I asked him if there is any news? He shook his head. "The same?" He nodded. "Is he still restless?" Mischa answered, "No; he is half unconscious". I nodded and turned away, and then Mischa said in a sort of agonised rush, "He does not open the eye". I looked at him and saw what agony he is in, but at once his face grew still again and when I left, almost at once, in case Mr. B. should telephone early, he smiled and said goodnight.

I realize that my present fears are all caused by Mischa. In reality nothing is changed since this morning, when he was a little better. I must remember this, and remember how his condition fluctuates.

Now I am going to bed.

October 29th

He died this morning, between 10.30 and 11.00

November 4th, 1949
Several days have passed, and I am going to make an account of them all in one.

I woke on Saturday morning, after an almost sleepless night, knowing that there was bad news. But Mrs. P. had promised to telephone early, as soon as she heard anything, so I did not obey my impulse to go at once to the flat for news. I dressed, drank my coffee and arranged my affairs so that I could spend the entire day, if necessary, at the flat. I felt as heavy as lead. Mrs. P. did not come till ten, and then told me that Gurdjieff was sinking, and the doctors thought he could not survive for more than a few hours. She asked me to go to the flat and stay there until told to do something else. At this point Mr. B. telephoned, thank goodness, so I gave him the news and he said he would come at once. I was terribly distressed that I had not told him sooner.

I went to the flat, where were Sofya Ivanovna, Emil, Lise (who had at last given in and was in bed in G.'s room, with a temperature) and various others. I finished cleaning the dining room and then on S.'s instructions went to clean the little ornaments on the 'Christmas tree' in the sitting room. While I was doing it, Emil came in, just after 11, sat down on a petit tabouret and said in a matter-of-fact voice, "Yes, Elizabeth, it's true. He did die." There was nothing to say, so I didn't say anything, but went on with my dusting. Emil went out, and came back a moment later with a glass of Armagnac. He said, "I brought you this, in case you feel cold". I was so touched by this, and amused at the same time: I thanked him and made him drink some too. I finished my job and went to the kitchen. Mme. Tracol arrived to look after Lise. She came straight to me and took my hands and said, "Remember, Elizabeth, this is for all of us; French, English and American. Remember. Remember we are all together."

Pierre telephoned from London about the Bennetts' arrival. I told him the news and asked him to tell Wolton.

I returned to the kitchen and helped Emil to prepare soup. People came in and out: Dr. Welch, Mme. de S., Tchechovich, George, Gabo . Dr. Welch sat in the kitchen and drank a big bowl of coffee. He said G. died most peacefully, after being for several hours unconscious. Dr. Welch said that at once, even before he died, all the stresses and lines of a sick man were gone from his face, and he was composed as he was in life. He said, "He died like a king".

He and the other doctors, nurses, etc., had said long before that he was unconscious, but Mme. de S. said she thought not, not till some time later. I believe her. When you really understand a person you know better than doctors. Apparently Mr. Gurdjieff made no secret of his own opinion with Dr. Welch. He told us that G. never deceived himself or the doctor about his position.

So I went, I suppose at about 1 p.m., to Le Bourget to meet the Bennetts. It was a beautiful clear sunny day.

Mr. B. went to the Hospital chapel, and later came to fetch Mrs. B. and me. We arrived at the chapel a little before six. I had not meant or wished to see his body; I had not intended to go to the chapel. But I got caught up in a sort of whirl of Bennetts, and was at the door of the chapel before I had time to protest. After a moment's thinking I decided to go in, and I am very thankful that I did.

I was overwhelmed by the force that came from him. One could not be near his body without feeling unmistakably his power. He looked magnificent; composed, content, *intentional*, for want of a better word. Not simply a body placed by someone else. He was undisguised, nothing was concealed from us. Everything belonging to him, his inner and outer life and all the circumstances and results of it, were there to be seen, if one could see. What force there was in him then! I have never seen anything in any way like it. This, I think, was what I had dreaded: I could not bear to see him with the force gone from him. Yet in fact I saw his power for the first time unobscured.

Several people stayed there all night. I returned about 6.15 on Sunday morning.

But this time everything was changed. Today I saw the peaceful face of a dead man. It might have been carved out of wood. I left and walked back to the hotel, knowing that now he was really gone, and I would not go to the chapel again.

People were arriving all the time from England and America. On Sunday evening about ten of us dined together and afterwards returned to the salon of the hotel, where Mr. B. talked to us. I had arranged to go with E.E.C. to the Hospital to show him the way. He was absorbed in listening to Mr. B., and I could not go without him. I stayed, but I was in an agony, I did

NOVEMBER 4TH

not know how to wait, I felt I *had* to go at the Hospital to see G. again. I don't know how I sat there; each minute seemed like an hour. But at last Mr. B. finished, and E. and I went in a taxi to Neuilly. My agonized impatience lasted until the very moment of reaching the doors of the chapel, where suddenly it was gone. I knew that I had come to look for something I should not find. Whatever it was was not there in the chapel. Indeed I felt there was more likelihood of finding it almost anywhere else. So I opened the door for E., and went away.

During these days I spent every morning at No. 6, cleaning, answering the telephone, etc. Usually 3 or 4 of the family came there for lunch.

Each day a service was held in the chapel at 3.30, and once or twice I stayed in the flat at that time so that Sofya Ivanovna could go. On Wednesday the body was brought, in its coffin, to the Russian Church in the Rue Daru, where psalms were sung between 5 and 6. The choir sang, as always, most beautifully.

I have forgotten to say that each day we had a reading in English from 'Beelzebub' at Mme. de S.'s flat. We read 'Purgatory' in two parts, and the third day, after the *mise en bière*, 'Form and Sequence' and 'Impartial Mentation', by fairly general request. After that third reading, we had glasses of tea and sandwiches. Mme. de S. spoke to us, quite shortly, about our immediate future plan of work. She spoke very powerfully.

So many other things I have not written here, too. Conversations and meetings and small happenings - dinner with the Bennetts at the Regence, lunch with Russell Page in Mr. G.'s café, an invitation for which I shall always be grateful to him, for shattering an imagination that I "could never go there again", the day I had to wait 3 hours in the Deux Magots, odd moments which will stay in my mind with Tchechovich, Page, Mr. B., Lise, Mrs. March. And one thing I shall always remember about this long week - the *cold*! I think I have never been so cold so continuously. It is my fault for bringing all the wrong clothes.

On Thursday was the funeral. We went to the Russian Church at 11.30. Flowers and incense and the most lovely music. The church was crowded, of course. We left, in buses and cars, for Avon at 2. He was buried between his mother and his wife.

Both in the church and at Avon I was filled for the first time, and, I think, the last, with the ordinary bitterness of loss. When I watched the candle burning away as I held it, when I looked down into the grave, I thought of all my life to be - not just got through, but spent - without him, and the burden seemed too great. Everything was made worse by Mr. B., who, suffering acutely himself, seemed to leave no detail undone which could add to my distress. By the evening, looking back over the day, I felt that a lifetime of future happiness could not compensate for the misery he caused me today - I felt I was paying all at once. I longed for Friday, when he and Mrs. B. would go back to England, and he would be able to lose himself in work and when I should be left in peace. I counted the hours till I could be alone.

However, it wasn't so bad in the end. We had coffee, and I kept my temper, and Wolton came to work at the rough draft which they both took round to Mme. de S. at 10.30. When they returned about 2.30 we went out to a place in the Champs Elysées for eggs and coffee and black bread and frankfurters. We had not eaten that day. I went to bed at a quarter to 7.

Mme. de S. asked me to stay on in Paris for a few days to do some work for her, so I went to Le Bourget with the Bennetts on Friday morning and returned to Paris in a taxi.

There were movements in the evening. Everyone wore their costumes, and Mme. de S. chose the numbers with great care. First No. 17,- then 19, 5, 36, 4, 39, 38, 34, 16 - I forget which others. We finished with 20 minutes of arms-out-sideways, audience included. Mme. de S. went straight through the movements without comment, although they were done unusually badly. There were many mistakes, and the whole effect, from the point of view of execution of the physical gestures, was ragged. Yet I have never known such feeling in them. At the end, she came forward from the piano and spoke to us, saying that we must work hard and come to the practices regularly, and that from next Monday we will begin to go through them all again, movement by movement. And how to work at them. Not in any way blaming us for our performances tonight, but saying how work must be from now on.

I am glad it is all over, the services and the funeral and the coming and going. What there is to be done is so tremendous, and when I look round at us who must do it I am very sure that we must lose no time. G. left no detail unattended to. Already it seems strange that we were all so blind to the real situation, and already there are wise people to say that they always knew. He provided so carefully for his family - the *château* was only one example - all those things. He arranged everything in the flat, saying that it must be kept just so for a museum; he told us that when "Beelzebub" was published his work would be finished - "then I can disappear", "then I can rest". And when Mr. B. said we would follow him wherever he went, he smilingly shook his head and said he might not be easy to follow; not easy to find him. All these things we disregarded, looking away to the other times, when he said, "I am Gurdjieff; I not will die" and when he said he would live to be 120, and all those things. I think he didn't mean us to understand. He could certainly have told us if he had wanted us to know. As it was we were able to behave naturally and normally until the very day he was taken to the Hospital, three days before he died. It is dreadful to think of the amount of suffering he must have had. All that so-called "*gaz*"! And the time he remarked with wonder that he had no pain. Yet he did not let himself go until his work was done, just as he did not wait when it was done. A whole year of such a teacher! It is strange to me that I have none of the bitterness of time wasted, but I have never once said to myself, "If only ... ", which I should have expected to say all day long. And I shall never have to think and speak theoretically, with "if". "*If* man could do such a thing; *if* there were this or that possibility for man". It *is* possible; I have seen it before my own eyes.

I do not feel the grief of losing a father or a friend or a teacher or any of the things he was to me. I am constantly reminded of his absence - yesterday I saw a man with a stick rather like him in figure, and had a momentary jolt: I see a Citroen going round the corner into the Rue des Colonels Renard, someone uses a familiar phrase, but all these things only remind me that his physical presence is gone. Inside myself I feel that he is here.

November 5th

B.C.M. and Emil stayed with me last night till 1.30 and this morning I slept right on till 9.45, when my breakfast came! I telephoned to Mme. de S., who said she would be passing the Rena in an hour or so and would I wait for her, which I did, but of course she did not come. Mrs. March, Madeleine, Emil and I had a picnic lunch together in Mrs. M.'s room - goat cheese, grapes, figs and coffee - and when Mrs. P. and Lord Pentland arrived at about 2.30. I returned to my room, not liking to go out in case Mme. de S. should come.

About 4 the bitter cold began to go, and by 5 it was raining hard. I lay on my bed and read 'Fragments' for an hour.

I must say about the Russian priest who took the daily services in the chapel at the Hospital, and afterwards conducted the burial service itself. Apparently he knew very little about Mr. Gurdjieff, but from the behaviour and general attitude of his people at the services he knew he must have been a remarkable man. It appears that he was much struck by this, so much so that he is going to preach a sermon about Mr. G. tomorrow in the Russian church. That is one way of bearing witness.

Mme. de Salzmann took her beginners' class of movements as usual at 7. I was once more filled with admiration of her teaching. What a wonderful woman.

I hurried away afterwards so that I could dine alone. I feel much better, after only one day of comparative peace: I no longer have to hold on with both hands to prevent myself from screaming, or at least, prevent myself from telling everyone the most unpleasant of my thoughts about them. When I returned, I talked for an hour to Mme. Barras, who made me laugh with her merciless gossip about her clients. Emil came to visit me, and also Mrs. March for a few minutes. To bed at about 11.30.

November 6th

I went early to the Rue du Bac and fetched the typing. I had about a dozen words with Mme. de S. - "Here are the two chapters". "Do you want four copies, as usual?" "Yes, four copies. Pay attention, there are some loose pages". "I will. Goodbye, Madame". "Goodbye, Elizabeth". A minute and a half? Two minutes? I feel better for the whole day.

I typed till it was time to go to church for the 12.30 service. Very short, only half an hour, but the *most* marvelous singing. The man who led the choir was leaning on his desk when we arrived, munching a *croissant*. When the service was about to start, he set down his *croissant* carefully on a handy piece of moulding, turned with unchanged gravity to his choir, threw back his head and produced these unearthly, astonishingly beautiful sounds. There were *many* people there. I saw Serge, Olivier and Anne-Marie in the charge of Mrs. March, and Marthe, with a black chiffon pinned over her hair. The church was crowded. Old Samson was there: I shook hands with him afterwards; he had no gloves and his hand was very cold.

I sneaked out down a little side street and lunched alone, returning to the typing at 1.45.

In the evening I went with Lord Pentland to the concert, and then we walked slowly back from the Rue Cardinet to the Rena, talking like mad. I had never really talked to him before, and I began to like him, which I did not in the past. Yvette played well. Bach and Mozart. It was strange and interesting to see her doing her own thing. She had always seemed to me faintly grotesque in appearance, with her inappropriately childish manner, her reedy little voice, funny lumpy figure, her thick spectacles and her primness. Tonight she still seemed like a child, but a self-possessed, sophisticated one. She went to the piano as though she were alone in her bedroom, going to the dressing table; she bowed like a well-behaved little girl giving a recitation. I enjoyed myself very much.

So back again. A slice of ham and a hard-boiled egg at the *café-tabac* on the corner and then back to 'Skridloff', I have done quite a lot today, in spite of interruptions. It is a bore to have to do my own checking and correcting; it takes a lot of time. At 12.15 I took pity on my neighbours and stopped typing. I went down for another gossip with Mme. Barras. She is a naughty old thing. It is rather awful to be so enamoured of my own company. I must try to be more sociable.

November 7th

This evening when we arrived at the flat for a reading at 8.30 and Mme. de S. said we would read in Mr. G.'s bedroom, as usual, I couldn't prevent a slight shock of distaste. But when we went in, the room was full of him still, and I was filled with happiness. It was as it has always been. Page sat in his armchair, and we read nearly the whole of Hadji Asvatz Troov. We were only a few, and all nations other than French: Page, Mrs. P., Emil, me, Keyserling and Dr. Welch. I had no regrets or agonies. In the street I expect him round every corner, but not in his own room. Is this very unfeeling of me? Surely it is better to feel positive happiness in his own place than to have morbid regrets? Anyway, if it is bad, then I am bad, because that is how I feel.

I typed quite a lot today (Karpenko) and checked Skridloff with Emil, had lunch with Mrs. M. and Mrs. P., movements practice with Solange in the evening - No. 1. Lord P. asked if l would be prepared to go to England for a few hours to give a message to Mr. Bennett, if he was unable to go himself. In the time it took me to say unhesitatingly, yes, I had seen it all: how I would deliver the message in Mr. B.'s office, have dinner alone and go to the lecture, stay at Coombe Springs and perhaps have a quick talk with Mr. B., and return to Paris in the morning ... But P. went himself after all!

So here I am, rather to my surprise, at the end of Volume 2 of this diary. How surprising that it should end as it does, with the death of our truly beloved and incomparable teacher, Mr. Gurdjieff. It is very touching to see how his loss affects the shop keepers of the Rue des Acacias, the flower woman who said was it true that the "*marchand de bon-bons*" is dead? And our own Mme. Charles, who was invited years ago to drink with him once in his café, and who remembers it as an outstanding event in her life. They wanted, she said, to invite him to tea with them one day, but they never did. "We never knew who he was", she said, "but of course we knew he was very learned"!

So now all that is over, and Volume 3 will be all about our struggles without him.

And what struggles they will be…

Printed in Great Britain
by Amazon